The TVRs

The TVRs

A collector's guide
by Graham Robson

MOTOR RACING PUBLICATIONS LTD
Unit 6, The Pilton Estate, 46 Pitlake, Croydon CR0 3RY, England

ISBN 0 947981 17 9
First published 1981
Second Edition 1987

Made and printed in Great Britain by
Adlard & Son Ltd The Garden City Press,
Letchworth, Herts. SG6 1JS

Contents

Introduction to first edition

When I set out to write this book, I intended it to be no more than a factual, blow-by-blow account of the way the TVR motor car has developed from the late-1950s to the present day. All that, I hope, *has* been included in the pages which follow, but an additional element has also crept in, repeatedly, and in the most unexpected places. This is what I can only define as the 'character' of the TVR, a quality with which all the cars have been liberally endowed.

Perhaps it would have been tidiest to start my story with the Grantura of 1958 and end it with the last M-Series car of 1979 — there are those cynics, for instance, who suggest that TVR have been building the same car for more than 20 years, and in *philosophy* they may be right — but I wanted to bring the story right up to date by describing the Tasmin model as well. What follows, therefore, is the factual story of the development of the TVR from 1958 to date, and I have tried very hard to cross-relate one car with another, and the links of one series with the next.

There has been at least one earlier book about TVR, which splendidly provided what I might describe as the human story behind the car itself. This *Collector's Guide,* however, is the first to provide the mass of statistics and identifying material that every true enthusiast needs to have when he is looking for a new car, or wants to restore his TVR to its original condition. The acknowledgements follow this introduction, but I should freely admit, right now, that I could not possibly have done the job without unlimited help from Martin Lilley and all his staff at Blackpool.

The first TVR went into production at about the same time that I first became involved with the motor industry, so you might say that we have both grown up in it and gained our experience together. I would be the first to admit, though, that the life and times of TVR has been infinitely more absorbing, and adventurous, than mine. However, the coincidence of dates, and my gradual conversion to a study of the industry's heritage, has let me keep a constant watch on the marque's progress.

It is a miracle that TVR still exists, for if all the laws of probability and finance had consistently applied to the marque it would have died some years ago. The original Granturas were crude machines built by an hilariously inexperienced team. For years, the marque stumbled from crisis to crisis, from boss to boss and from one set of capital to the next. TVR Engineering was displaced by Layton Sports Cars, TVR Cars took over from that, and Grantura Engineering kept the pot sporadically boiling until it slid into bankruptcy in 1965. It needed Arthur and Martin Lilley — father and son — to make the bold move of buying up the assets, such as they were, breathe life into the corpse, set up TVR Engineering Ltd, and bring about the revival which has continued, not without problems, to the present day.

Before the Lilley influence took hold, there had only truly been one type of TVR which, one chassis change and several engine options later, was still a rather unreliable machine. It was only after stability set in, towards the end of the 1960s, that the really remarkable advances in engineering, performance and product quality began to occur. It was all part of a complete change of image. Before Lilley, there was always the feeling in TVR-watchers' minds that the firm might collapse; after Lilley, as it were, that feeling was replaced by one of permanence.

The character of the TVR has always shone through, and this is nowhere more obvious than in its engineering. Each and every TVR has had a multi-tubular chassis-frame and all-independent suspension; each and every TVR has had a glass-fibre bodyshell. Every car, too, whether endowed with a powerful engine or not, has undeniably been a sports car, and you could never accuse TVR of providing boring machines, even if they were not all very fast.

More than 5,000 glass-fibre-bodied TVRs have been made, and the Blackpool-based company has now completed a major investment and introduced a range of new Tasmins to see it well into the 1980s. It is a marque which has merited serious statistical study for some time, and I am very happy to have been able to tackle the job. Somewhere in these pages — whether in the form of a Griffith or a Vixen, a Turbo Convertible or a Ford-engined Grantura, there may be a TVR for you. But don't all shout at once — the supply is limited!

GRAHAM ROBSON

Acknowledgements

When I started researching material for this book, I thought that fact-gathering for what is, in effect, a 25-year history would be straightforward enough. I was wrong. It needed a great deal of effort, and I needed a lot of help before I was satisfied that all available knowledge gaps had been filled.

My job, therefore, has been made a lot easier by the following experts:

For encouragement, for their personal efforts with the archives, for raking back into their memories, and for reading the manuscript progressively as it took shape: Martin Lilley, Stewart Halstead, Carole Newton and Stan Kilcoyne, of TVR Engineering Ltd.

For their enthusiasm in maintaining interest in the marque through thick and thin: The TVR Car Club, and particularly Douglas Manuel, the Secretary, for his advice.

For his personal involvement, in business and pleasure, with TVR, and for his immense stock of historical records and illustrations: John Bailie and his staff at Image Publicity in Blackpool.

For his forebearance, as usual, and for his encyclopaedic knowledge of *Autocar's* pictorial archive: Warren Allport, Assistant Editor.

Apart from TVR Engineering Ltd and Image Publicity, for providing photographs: *Autocar, Thoroughbred & Classic Cars, Motor* and Douglas Manuel.

Those recorders of the motoring scene, for their archival importance: *Autocar, Motor, Autosport, Thoroughbred & Classic Cars* and *Road & Track.*

My personal American connection: Richard Langworth, of Dragonwyck Publishing Inc, New Hampshire, USA.

Lastly, of course, I should acknowledge yet again the debt which all TVR enthusiasts owe to Arthur and Martin Lilley for their faith in the marque. If they had not bought up the thrice bankrupt remains of TVR in 1965 it would almost certainly have died there and then, and this story would never have had to be written. Even since then, there have been as many hard knocks as there have been easy successes, and I admire them all the more for that. Through their persistence, I am sure that TVR will prosper for many years to come.

GRAHAM ROBSON

Introduction to second edition

A lot has happened to TVR since this book was originally published, and I am delighted to bring the story right up to date. Not only did the company change hands in 1982, when Peter Wheeler took control and Stewart Halstead became managing director, but many new models have appeared, sales have increased, and the prospects for the 1990s are encouraging.

I am grateful to Peter Wheeler, Stewart Halstead, Mike Penny, Noel Palmer and Carole Newton —all of TVR — for helping me to bring the story up to date and providing all the new illustrations, and to Giles Cooper of the TVR Centre for giving me so much advice on the little ways of more modern TVRs as they grow old.

January 1987

GRAHAM ROBSON

By 1956, two years after the first TVR had been sold, this predecessor of the Grantura had evolved. Beneath the skin are the chassis, suspensions and Coventry Climax engine first seen in Trevor Wilkinson's Jomar design, but the bodyshell was fashioned by TVR utilizing a Rochdale proprietary rear-end and adding a nose of similar shape. Jack Pickard, one of Wilkinson's early associates, is at the wheel of this car, which was intended for competition use, hence the closed-in passenger space and the combined headrest/fairing. *(John Bailie)*

CHAPTER 1

Ancestors and parentage

Prototypes and specials

The story of TVR effectively begins in 1947, for it was in that year that a young man called Trevor Wilkinson built his first 'special'. However, the first-ever car which Wilkinson dubbed a TVR did not follow until 1949, and the first TVRs built in series — a very limited series — were not put on the market until 1954.

Trevor Wilkinson was born in Blackpool in 1923 and left school in 1937, at 14 years of age, with no specific engineering knowledge. He then joined a local garage to serve his apprenticeship as a mechanic and stayed in Blackpool throughout the war years, helping in the family business (a shop selling baby's prams) for some time. In 1946, with no more experience and mechanical training than he had picked up in his teens in the motor trade, the young Wilkinson determined to set up shop on his own. At the age of 23, therefore, and in spite of some parental opposition, he acquired an old wheelwright's shop in Blackpool and established Trevcar Motors. Not only did the tiny business take on car repairs, along with the buying and selling of cars, but it became involved in a variety of light engineering enterprises.

In 1947, Wilkinson owned an old Alvis Firebird — a four-cylinder car of no particular engineering merit which had been built in Coventry during the 1930s — and it was on this basis that he built up his first 'special'. The rolling chassis was not altered, though the standard body (which presumably was on its last legs anyway) was discarded, and a new light-alloy two-seater sports car was built to take its place.

Later that year, TVR Engineering replaced Trevcar Motors, Wilkinson was joined by Jack Pickard, and their collective enthusiasm turned to the idea of building a sports car which would be 'special' from the ground up. Giving it a name — the initials TVR came by shortening TreVoR's christian name — was easy enough, but designing and building the car was not. The original TVR was not on the road until 1949 and the third car in this embryo series was not completed until 1951.

It is important, at this point, to realize that neither Trevor Wilkinson nor Jack Pickard had any formal engineering training. Neither had formal education which went beyond the minimum requirements of the state — which meant that they had left school at 14 years of age — and neither had had any experience or knowledge of the way in which cars were normally designed. Factors such as weight distribution, spring rates and damper settings, and costing for series production were completely foreign to them. They knew no more than they had learned from looking at other cars — some which they liked, some which they did not like — and from reading about them in the motoring publications of the day.

In 1949, therefore, with a great deal of enthusiasm but little money, Wilkinson set out to design and build his first car, which was based around a multi-tubular chassis, of which the upper tubes also supported the body skin panels. There was trailing-link independent front suspension, coil springs from the crash bumpers of fairground bumper cars, a Morris Eight rear axle and a side-valve 1,172-cc Ford 100E engine and its matching three-speed gearbox. Except for the tubular chassis and the skin panels, every component was secondhand. The panel-beater who had built the Alvis Firebird's body, Les Dale, produced a two-seater 'torpedo'-style shell for the new car, which used Morris Eight Series E road wheels and had cycle-type wings.

Having built the car, Wilkinson then sold it to his cousin for

The first TVR properly to be put on sale was the multi-tube-framed car introduced in 1954. This version, complete with an RGS Atalanta glass-fibre bodyshell, was known as the TVR Sports Saloon. The chassis used many Austin A40 Somerset components, and Trevor Wilkinson originally intended the cars to be supplied with A40 1,200-cc engines as well. However, about 20 chassis were supplied between 1954 and 1956 with a variety of engines, the most powerful the 2½-litre twin-high-camshaft Lea-Francis unit. *(John Bailie)*

£325 and immediately set about building another. The second car was very similar to the first, except that it was treated to coil-spring-and-wishbone independent front suspension from the current Austin A40 Devon saloon, and the third car, which followed in 1951, not only had the A40's front suspension, but also that model's 1.2-litre pushrod ohv engine, four-speed gearbox and spiral-bevel back axle; rear suspension, as before, was by half-elliptic leaf springs, with no extra location. The third car was used for a time in local competitions, driven by Wilkinson, and it won several awards.

By now, the sports car 'bug' had well and truly taken hold of Wilkinson and TVR Engineering. In 1953, Trevor Wilkinson settled down to design a new car — not merely a 'special', but one which he intended to sell in a series. Although it was obviously and directly descended from the layout of the original three cars, the new TVR, which went on sale in 1954, was different in almost every detail.

One of the first-ever multi-tubular backbone chassis designs, of 1955, fitted with a light-alloy Coventry Climax overhead-camshaft engine, and destined for Ray Saidel in Manchester, New Hampshire, in the United States. This was the first TVR to have independent front *and* rear suspensions, and Saidel bodied them and called them Jomars. This was the obvious and true original ancestor of the Grantura. *(John Bailie)*

Front view of the 1955-style backbone-chassis layout produced by TVR for sale to Ray Saidel. This was intended to be bodied as a Jomar sports-racing car and has a Coventry-Climax engine fitted. Both front and rear suspension links are those used at the front of the VW Beetle. Note the low position of the water-cooling radiator, the light-alloy bolt-on road wheels and the racing tyres. *(John Bailie)*

As did so many other aspirant car manufacturers of the 1950s, Wilkinson decided to offer his cars as complete and built-up machines, ready-to-assemble kits, or even little more than chassis-frames. In other words, he was quite happy to supply exactly what his customers demanded, for it was in this way that he hoped to expand. In particular, he decided to source as many as possible of the mechanical components from one mass-produced model, and he decided that it made no economic sense to build his own light-alloy bodies. The car he chose to provide many mechanical parts was the Austin A40 (by now, incidentally, rebodied and called the Somerset) and for bodies he resolved to buy in whatever he needed.

The 1954 variety of TVR, therefore, was based on a new design of multi-tubular chassis-frame (something like that of the 'X' type of Allards), with upper and lower tubular longitudinals and vertical, horizontal or diagonal cross-bracings where appropriate. It was by no means a pure spaceframe (Colin Chapman, no doubt, would have laughed very loudly if he had bothered to analyze the stresses in the structure) but Wilkinson had never intended that it should be; instead, it was solid, simple and neatly made. The independent coil-sprung front suspension, wheels and spiral-bevel back axle were all from the Austin A40 (and were bought from the local BMC dealer in Blackpool), while the rack-and-pinion steering was from a Morris Minor. Most of the chassis tubes were of 1.5-inch diameter, with 16-gauge walls — a cross-section to be used by TVR models built until the present day and to be found even in the Tasmin of the 1980s.

Because of the way in which the car was sold, there was really no such thing as a standard engine, although Wilkinson originally intended that the 1,200-cc Austin A40 engine and gearbox should be just that. In rather more than two years and about 20 cars or chassis, A40, Ford 100E, MG TF 1500, MGA or even 2½-litre Lea Francis engines and transmissions were used.

For their bodies, TVR went to firms already catering for such a demand. The sleek fastback coupe styles, now known as TVR Sports Saloons, had glass-fibre bodyshells by RGS Atalanta, while other open shells were provided by Rochdale and Microplas. The Sports Saloons were advertised for sale at £650 (plus Purchase Tax if completely assembled), though only three were delivered.

While this sporadic activity was taking place and TVR Engineering was still paying its way in Blackpool with engineering work connected with the vast entertainment industry which dominated the sea front between Lytham St Anne's and Fleetwood, Trevor Wilkinson was already making plans for yet another type of car, this time more advanced, sportscar-like and specialized than before. To TVR enthusiasts, it was important for two main reasons — it had a backbone-style frame and the first TVR-built glass-fibre bodyshell. It was also the first TVR to be built in the company's 'new' premises.

In the meantime, Wilkinson had been amazed to receive an order for a rolling chassis from one Ray Saidel, of Manchester, New Hampshire, USA, which according to the order, should be fitted with a Coventry Climax FWA light-alloy engine of the type which was already making its name as a sports-car racing unit in Britain and Europe. It was to be the start of a fruitful, if turbulent, relationship.

Wilkinson's aim, with his new chassis design, was to lower the

seats and, therefore, the entire car. This would not only improve the aerodynamics, but also improve the roadholding. With the existing chassis, the height of the seats was determined by the fact that they had to sit on top of the floor of the bought-in bodies, which were themselves perched on the tubular frame.

The new chassis, therefore, was laid out as a basic backbone type (though it is doubtful if Wilkinson called it anything as scientific as that, at least, not at first). Instead of having widely spaced longitudinal members, its structure was based around an open box-section of four tubular longitudinal members, which were swept closer together (and the top tubes lowered) to provide an acceptable section through the cockpit. The engine and transmission, therefore, were completely wrapped around with steel tubes, suitably braced and reinforced to increase the beam and torsional properties, and the frame itself started and finished at the front and rear suspension mountings. There were outrigging tubes, of course, along the level of the straight bottom tubes, and the result was that the seats could be mounted right down at floor level, about six inches, no more, from ground level.

This, too, was the first TVR with independent front *and* rear suspension. Once again, Wilkinson was anxious to use as many as possible of the chassis components from the same model and since there was no British car with the sort of layout he needed, he turned to foreign models. For the new frame, and for the design which was to be used on all TVRs built between 1957 and 1962, he chose trailing-link front and rear suspension, sprung on transverse torsion bars, and he took his assemblies from the VW Beetle. Note that front *and* rear TVR suspensions used the trailing links and transverse torsion bar of the Beetle's front suspension, for the Beetle's rear-end was a swing-axle layout to match its rear-mounted engine.

The rolling chassis for Ray Saidel was soon given a USA-built bodyshell and named a Jomar (after JOhn and MARgaret, Saidel's two children), and more orders for this all-independent chassis followed. Out of this design came the original (pre-Grantura) TVR Coupe of which, illogically enough, three closed and three open examples were to be built. Unlike the original Saidel car, which had VW-type wheels to suit the VW brakes and suspension, the Coupes had 11-inch Girling brakes and Dunlop 48-spoke wire wheels, but all were fitted with Coventry Climax engines, backed by MGA gearboxes.

The body style for this car evolved by the most classic cut-and-shut methods, originally from a Rochdale shell, and with a front-end modelled on the Rochdale's rear-end, it did not at first look like what was to become the 'classic' TVR coupe style, as a notchback roof, on rather conventional lines, was chosen. However, gradually and inexorably, these hand-to-mouth projects were all leading towards a definitive TVR design, for by 1957 certain of the basic dimensions had already settled into place. The 1957 Coupes, like the Granturas which were to follow, had established the backbone frame, all-independent trailing-arm suspensions, VW worm-and-sector steering, a 7-ft 0-in wheelbase, 4-ft 4-in front and rear tracks, and the classic early-Grantura overall dimensions of 11-ft 6-in length, 5-ft 4-in width and 4-ft 0-in height.

In the meantime, at the beginning of 1956, Wilkinson had sold the original Trevcar/TVR Engineering building at Beverley Grove, Blackpool, and taken a long lease on part of a redundant brickworks on the Hoo Hill Industrial Estate, at Layton, also in the outskirts of Blackpool. By this time, too, Bernard Williams had become a director of the company, and extra finance had been provided by Fred Thomas, of Bolton. It was the start of an expansion in business activity which would eventually prove to be fatal to the original concern. The final nudge, from the building of cars in tiny quantities to the building of TVRs in something like series production, followed in 1957, when Ray Saidel exhibited a car at the 1957 New York Auto Show (having been appointed the first-ever TVR/Jomar distributor) and was astonished to receive a flood of orders, few of which the company could possibly fulfil.

Working on ideas suggested to them by Saidel (one of which was that he would like to be able to offer a sleeker, fastback model), and with an idea of shaking down the backbone frame design into more of a series-production model, Wilkinson and Jack Pickard set to work on what was to become the first true production TVR. For 1958, therefore, a new era at TVR was beginning. With Wilkinson as managing director and technical chief, Jack Pickard at his elbow, Bernard Williams effectively heading the sales effort and Fred Thomas providing finance, TVR Engineering faced up to an exciting future. At that moment, no-one could possibly have guessed that there would be a complete financial reconstruction within 12 months, a bankruptcy within five years and a further bankruptcy only three years after that. For the founding fathers of TVR, not only was it going to be an exciting ride, but a bumpy one, too!

CHAPTER 2

Grantura Marks I, II and IIA

1958 to 1962

The series-production TVR Coupe, which was not christened 'Grantura' at that stage, but retrospectively became known as such, was revealed in 1958, at a time when only one representative car had been completed. *The Autocar* and *The Motor* made mention of the launch and clearly the two long-established weekly magazines attended the same press briefing for they both emphasized that the launch was the successful culmination of a couple of years of development, testing and racing (by Ray Saidel and others in North America), that Trevor Wilkinson and Bernard Williams were the two most important individuals in the Blackpool company's team and that a choice of alternative engines would be made available. Interestingly enough, at this point the prices quoted were for complete cars, though TVR always made it clear that they were prepared to supply kits, indeed that they would supply cars to which the customers could fit their own engines if they wished.

Their launch got off to a flying start because the prototype was displayed for a time in the Manchester showroom of H. & J. Quick Ltd, the prestigious Ford dealers, at which time a white lie was told to the effect that: 'So far, a batch of 10 has been produced . . .', when, as already made clear, the only complete TVR was the one on display in the showroom in Manchester.

The Autocar set the seal of respectability on the Grantura (which had received its official title by then) by becoming the first magazine to publish a detailed technical analysis of the car. On March 6, 1959, not only did they devote three pages to the Grantura, but they graced it with one of their famous cutaway drawings to illustrate the complexities of the backbone chassis.

The Mark I, like all Granturas built until mid-1962, was based

on the multi-tubular chassis-frame which Trevor Wilkinson had begun to design in 1955, and which had first been supplied (to Ray Saidel, for use as a Jomar) in 1956. The engine bay, enclosed by the chassis backbone tubes, the front suspension cross-members and the glass-fibre bulkhead, was roomy enough to accept several different engines. At first there was really no such thing as a 'standard' engine, though *The Autocar's* description was of a car equipped with a 1,216-cc Coventry Climax FWE engine (with an MGA gearbox). Other engines offered, and fitted from time to time, were the obsolescent side-valve 1,172-cc Ford 100E unit, which was matched by the three-speed gearbox found in the Anglia and Prefect saloons; a supercharged (by Shorrock) version of this; the new overhead-valve, over-square, 997-cc Ford 105E engine and four-speed gearbox from the 1960-model Ford Anglia; and the 1,489-cc MGA engine and four-speed gearbox.

The kernel of the Grantura's design was the use of VW trailing-link independent suspension at front *and* rear. Twin parallel trailing links were employed at each corner of the car, joined — top and bottom — by laminated torsion bars enclosed in the transverse frame cross-members. The bars were anchored at their centre by bolts screwed into the centre of the tubes, and were effectively short stiff bars mounted end-to-end in the same tube. Incidentally, although this was a VW system through and through, the patriotic *Autocar,* in January 1958, had chosen to describe the trailing arms as 'recalling the Atalanta system', and the torsion bars as being like those of the defunct Daimler Conquest/Lanchester Leda models!

The suspension on the TVR was so stiff that no anti-roll bars were needed and the telescopic dampers must have had quite an

Side view of one of the early series-production Grantura Mark I models, showing the stubby and completely characteristic lines, the wrap-around rear window, the smoothly contoured tail (contrasting with the lumpy outline of the 1959 Coupé) and the lack of opening quarter-windows in the doors. Already, however, modifications have been made to the original, for this particular car has exposed headlamps with chrome decorating rings. *(John Bailie)*

the same as those fitted to the Austin-Healey 100-Six, but not to the Austin-Healey 3000, which had discs), and bi-metal Alfin drums were specified, as were Dunlop centre-lock wire-spoke wheels, also of Austin-Healey type. Even in 1959, when *The Autocar's* analysis was published, it was stated that Girling front discs would soon replace the drums and that ventilated disc wheels would soon be standardized (with a £35 price reduction). In the event, the disc wheels were never used and the use of disc brakes was delayed until 1961, and the advent of the Grantura Mark IIA.

Other mechanical fittings included a cross-flow water radiator, mounted well forward and low down in the nose, an 8¾-gallon fuel tank (TVR-manufactured) centrally mounted behind the line

easy time. The geometry meant that the wheels rolled at the same rate as the chassis and bodyshell, which is to say that the effectiveness of the tyres decreased as the roll increased. With such hard suspension, however, there was undoubtedly very little roll, even at high cornering speeds. The rest of the front suspension and steering was an ingenious amalgam of standard items — something for which TVR became noted as the years progressed — for although the kingpin was a light-alloy item manufactured by TVR, the stub-axle was from a BMC (Austin A55) saloon, the brakes were as used on the current Austin-Healey 100-Six and the steering box was a Ford item. At the rear, the same basic kingpins were used, but the toe-in was controlled by the fitment of extra radius-arms, which were really track rods fixed securely to the chassis at the inner ends; these could be adjusted for length in the normal way, an operation made necessary by the fitting of Metalastik bushes in the kingpins and rubber bushes at the track rod end.

Girling 11-inch diameter drum brakes were standard (virtually

Parked in typically industrial North Country surroundings, this early Grantura Mark I shows off its very smooth front-end styling, which had never been near a wind-tunnel, but was demonstrably efficient and wind-cheating. One tiny badge on the nose was all that advertised the TVR make. The wipers have yet to be fitted to this car. Note the huge expanse of bonnet combined with the front wings, which was front-hinged and swung up to provide unrivalled access to the engine and front suspension. *(John Bailie)*

This 1958-9 Grantura Mark I is waiting to be shipped to the United States, though it has been built in right-hand-drive form. Obvious in this shot are features so typical of TVRs for many years to come, including the panoramic rear window, the smooth lines, the very short rear overhang and the lack of access to the rear stowage space. Somewhere in there was the spare wheel, which had to be extracted through the passenger compartment and one of the doors! The quarter-bumpers were more for visual effect than for protection. *(John Bailie)*

of the rear suspension/final-drive unit, and the spare wheel tucked well down in the tail, behind the tank, and covered by interior trim. No matter which engine/gearbox combination was chosen, the Grantura's chassis-mounted differential/final-drive was the BMC B-Series hypoid-bevel design (as fitted, from the mid-1950s, to cars as diverse as the MGA and the Austin-Morris Farina-styled saloons), with a variety of ratios which depended on the revving capacity of the engine chosen, but the case was a light-alloy TVR design.

It was the Grantura's looks, however, which made the initial impression on a potential customer. TVR might have started from the unlikely base of Rochdale styling and used hit-and-miss, cut-and-fill, methods of arriving at the final shape, but the end result was undeniably distinctive, even if the designers would have liked it to look longer and even more wind-cheating. It was, in fact, the basic shape from which all TVRs built until the end of

the 1970s would evolve and it stood the passage of time remarkably well.

The choice of glass-fibre production was almost inevitable, for no British manufacturer could produce hand-built metal shells for anything except an expensive car, and at the rate of production forecast by TVR there was no chance of having pressed panels. It was a simple fastback shell, with no access to the stowage space from outside the car (which made removal of the spare wheel a tricky and time-wasting process — not to mention hard work), but with a full-width bonnet moulding hinged at the front of the chassis-frame and giving almost ideal access to the engine bay and front suspension.

The windscreen was that of a Ford Consul/Zephyr Mark II — available in either toughened or laminated glass — while the large curved rear window was Perspex, and special to TVR. On the first cars, the lines were extremely smooth, as the headlamps were faired in (like those of the 1957 Coupes), and there were no

Production of tubular chassis-frames at the Hoo Hill works in Blackpool. These four frames represent up to two weeks' complete production of TVRs, for output at the end of the 1950s was still extremely limited. Many changes were made to this design before it gave way to the coil-sprung Mark III frame of 1962. *(John Bailie)*

quarter windows in the doors. One considerable disadvantage, which was not to be alleviated for some years, was that the doors were extremely short, which made access to the seats rather difficult, though the driving position itself was very comfortable.

In the first year, TVR found it difficult to produce the Granturas at the rate which Ray Saidel demanded. After the phenomenal interest showed in the prototype car at the 1957 New York Auto Show, Saidel was convinced that he could sell just as many Granturas as TVR could deliver. Their problem, however, was not only that they were still learning how to build glass-fibre coupe bodies in quantity *and* to the appropriate level of constructional quality, but they were also finding the usual financial problems connected with the rapid expansion of a small business.

By the end of 1958, with less than two dozen cars built in all,

From the rear, the original type of TVR chassis can be seen to be very low and squat. The final-drive housing was special for this car, but the rear suspension was from the front of a VW Beetle. This chassis would eventually have gone to the United States to become a racing Jomar. *(John Bailie)*

A detail of the rear suspension and drive-shaft layout of the early-type trailing-arm TVR chassis. The trailing arms and the transverse torsion bars are from a VW Beetle front suspension, though the drive-shafts are special, as is the cast-alloy rear-suspension upright. *(John Bailie)*

TVR Engineering found themselves with plenty of orders, but with a large and growing cash-flow crisis. The result was that TVR Engineering was wound up in December 1958 and a new company, Layton Sports Cars Ltd, was formed to take over the business. The car itself, the premises in which it was built, and the principals (Wilkinson and Williams) were not changed, but there was a change in financial backing. Shortly after this, early in 1959, another company, Grantura Engineering Ltd, was also formed, and in a very complex legal and financial situation, they took over much of the purchase and manufacturing responsibilities from Layton Sports Cars, though the two companies operated from the same premises; Layton, indeed, was the 'front' organization which took all the publicity.

Early in 1959, when *The Autocar* published its technical analysis, the car had changed significantly in detail, and it was

The ancient but sturdy design of side-valve Ford engine — the 1,172-cc Type 100E unit — which powered some of the original Grantura Mark Is. This was Ford's own installation, and for TVR use a different gear-change was adopted. Some 100E engines were supercharged, but it was still not the most powerful and satisfactory way to power a TVR — the Coventry Climax engine was best for that. *(Ford Motor Company)*

stated that: 'Of the 30 or so TVRs so far made, some two dozen are in America', and it was also made clear that the American cars were being sold as Jomars. An early example of TVR optimism was evident, for the factory had assured *The Autocar* that: 'Present production rate is about six cars a month, but the rate is rising steadily and is planned to reach about five a week by the end of this year'; what actually happened is that production slowed down during 1959 as the outstanding orders either disappeared, or tailed off.

In the meantime, the headlamps had come out into the open, swivelling quarter windows had been added to the doors, which made the drop glasses even narrower than before, and flares had been added above the front wheelarches and wings, the flares actually being part of the lift-up bonnet moulding. Twin 'nostril' vents were to be found in the bonnet, above the main radiator air intake, on some cars and during 1959 small vents were added behind the front wheelarches, which helped to channel hot air out of the engine bay (particularly on the most powerful Climax-

Two views of the 1,588-cc BMC MGA 1600 engine and transmission which was used to power many of the Grantura Marks I, II and IIA built between 1958 and 1962. Early examples had 1,489-cc engines, which were slightly less powerful and had minor visual differences. Most of the lengthy transmission casing houses the output shaft and the complex but precise gear-change linkage. Some Granturas were treated to the HRG-Derrington conversion of this engine, which included a light-alloy cross-flow cylinder-head. (BL)

Many older TVRs now on the market will inevitably have been 'customized', rather like this Mark I Grantura, which features bonnet straps, wing mirrors and the engine bay air vents and front wing flares which had been added to the specification in 1959. This car also has the door quarter-windows fitted to all but the first cars and the rather more substantial bumpers which soon became a feature of the design. *(John Bailie)*

engined cars).

At this stage in the development of the TVR production car, the specification was often altered to suit the individual customer's requirements. The fact, therefore, that bonnet air vents were only supposed to be on Ford-engined cars at first didn't mean that they were never found on cars with other engines. It was also possible for a customer to order a lightweight bodyshell, so that he could race the car, though this, like all the others, was bonded to the multi-tube frame on assembly, which made things awkward (and more expensive) when crash repairs became necessary.

Among the special fittings found on early Granturas (many of which, of course, may now have been taken out of the cars which still survive) were the Stage 2 or even Stage 3 tuning kits on Climax-engined cars, some of which were of 1,098-cc, to race in the 1,100-cc classes, and some were the 1,216-cc (FWE) units found in all 1959-63 Lotus Elites and several other specialist sports cars of the period. It was also possible to order the KSK four-speed gearbox conversion for Ford 100E engine/gearbox models *(The Autocar's* 1959 description mentions this), and by

1960 it was also possible to ask for Girling front wheel disc brakes at extra cost.

There is only limited scope in a *Collector's Guide* for discussion of the commercial events which affected the evolution of a marque, or a particular model. However, it should be pointed out that Layton Sports Cars' financial affairs often seemed to be in disarray, with production *and* orders fluctuating considerably from season to season. In 1959, this resulted in Ray Saidel relinquishing his TVR dealership in North America, which therefore meant the death of the Jomar and the loss of the US market to TVR for some time. Several individuals (including financier Fred Thomas) moved out, but an ex-Rolls-Royce engineer called John Thurner joined the company as its new technical chief, taking over from the car's originator, Trevor Wilkinson, who was gradually pushed further into the background.

However, although only 54 cars were built in the 18 months leading up to the end of 1959, the total production run of TVR Granturas was brought up to exactly 100 by mid-1960, at which time the rate of production was increasing markedly and the Mark

My, how you've changed! This shot, taken in 1976, gives a vivid and revealing comparison between the current model TVR 3000M Turbo and a 1961 Grantura Mark IIA. The family resemblance is clear, though it is quite obvious that there is no direct link between the two designs. The Mark IIA has been modified by its owner, for the single bonnet air intake was never part of the standard specification. This picture was taken outside the TVR factory at Bristol Avenue. *(TVR)*

Arnold Burton competing in the 1961 Tulip Rally, high up in the mountains of France, in his Mark II Grantura. He finished, but only just, as he was classified last of all. *(John Bailie)*

I was superseded by the Mark II.

The Grantura Mark II was effectively a lightly modified Mark I, with several improvements and a little visual retouching. The rolling chassis was basically unchanged and the bodyshell itself was virtually untouched. This time it was the turn of *The Motor* to describe the latest car (in their issue of July 6, 1960), when the realignment of mechanical offerings and the styling changes were clarified.

The principal engine was now the MGA unit, a few early cars having the now-obsolete 1,489-cc capacity, but most having the 1,588-cc MGA 1600 capacity which, in 80-bhp form, had been used on MGAs built from mid-1959. The standard options were the 997-cc Ford 105E unit, or the Type FWE 1,216-cc Coventry Climax engine.

Visually, the flared front wheelarches of the later Mark Is were now matched by flares over the rear wheel cut-outs and the rear wings themselves had been reshaped and extended (almost becoming small fins in the process) and were treated to different (standard Lucas) tail-lamps and separate flashing indicators. The same type of amber indicators were also fixed to the bonnet panel,

The 1,216-cc Coventry Climax Type FWE single-cam engine was a snug fit in the engine bay of the Mark II Grantura. This was *Autocar's* road-test car of 1961 which, with 83 bhp, returned a maximum speed of 101 mph. Details clear in this picture include the location of the radiator header tank, which is behind and above the engine, and the prominence of the cross-tube of the chassis-frame, which housed the transverse torsion bar of the independent front suspension. Tiny bonnet holding-down straps were fitted to this particular car. *(Autocar)*

behind and at each corner of the nostril intakes.

All the optional extras developed for the Grantura Mark I were carried forward, except that the side-valve Ford engine was no longer available as it was both underpowered and out of production.

The Mark II, not only an improved Grantura but a more popular one, achieved higher sales than the Mark I in the first few months, yet it was made obsolete by the Mark IIA of early-1961. The reference to Mark IIA, however, meant very little, except that Girling front disc brakes were standardized, the engine line-up was modified yet again and the door quarter windows could no

longer be opened.

In previous TVR books there has been confusion about the availability of the Ford Classic 1,340-cc engine, for it has been stated that this became available towards the end of Mark II production. This, however, cannot possibly be so, for the Classic itself was not revealed until May 1961, the option of the engine was not publicized until September 1961, and by this time the Mark II had been replaced by the Mark IIA.

In the meantime, the standard MGA engine had been enlarged yet again so, allowing for the fact that the first few Mark IIAs were built with 1,588-cc MGA 1600 engines, the available

22

engines on Mark IIAs were the MGA 1600 Mark II unit of 1,622 cc, the ubiquitous Coventry Climax FWE engine (still standard, of course, in the Lotus Elite), one or two Ford 105E engines and — from the early autumn of 1961 — the 109E 1,340-cc Ford Classic engine, which was merely a long-stroke derivative of the 105E unit.

Even on this broad base of 'standard' options, however, there could be further variation if the customer so desired it. MGA engines could be supplied with the HRG-Derrington light-alloy cross-flow cylinder-head (which was eventually homologated and was used not only on cars in rallying, but on the 1962 Le Mans cars described in the next chapter), while Coventry Climax-engined cars could be supplied with the ZF gearbox of the type already available with the same engine in the Lotus Elite. Another mechanical oddity was that while the Ford-type worm-and-sector steering was retained for most cars, rack-and-pinion steering was made available for those cars fitted with the Coventry Climax

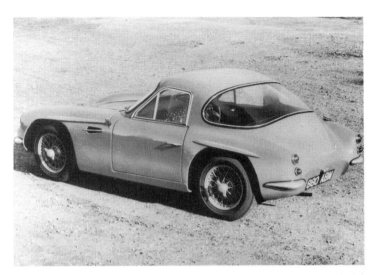

Three-quarter-rear view of *Autocar's* Grantura Mark IIA road-test car, the first officially tested TVR to exceed 100 mph. The bonnet straps (at the tail of the lift-up bonnet moulding) were non-standard. *(Autocar)*

This picture of *Autocar's* Mark IIA Grantura road-test car of November 1961 demonstrates the small door aperture which was a feature of all short-wheelbase TVRs built before 1967. This particular car was fitted with a Coventry Climax Type FWE 1,216-cc engine. *(Autocar)*

engine. Precise steering, it seems, was only considered essential if the highest-performance model was being ordered. . . .

In the meantime, further financial and organizational changes had taken place. During 1961, TVR appointed Dick Monnich, of New York, to distribute their cars in North America, while from September of that year, control of Layton Sports Cars was taken over by Brian Hopton and Keith Aitchison, whose Aitchison-Hopton business in Chester was already a leading TVR outlet. Hopton became chairman and managing director, and set about living and working in a style to which all previous TVR directors would have liked to have been accustomed. It was not at all clear, however, whether such conspicuous expenditure would be for the long-term benefit of TVR — or Hopton himself. There was no change in company name, and no immediate change in the TVR production car itself.

Action study of a Coventry Climax-engined Grantura Mark IIA, which shows just how hard was the suspension of the early cars, for this car is just about on the limit of adhesion, a fact demonstrated by the shape of the outside front tyre. The ground clearance is very limited — a characteristic of almost all early TVRs. *(Autocar)*

The last of the Mark IIAs, however, was eventually to be built in September 1962, some months after the car which was to replace it had been announced, raced and stumblingly had found its way into production. Mark IIs and Mark IIAs were in production for just over two years, during which period about 400 cars were sold — by far the fastest selling rate of the TVR so far, and four times as many sales as of the Grantura Mark I.

The new Mark III chassis and suspension systems were very different from those used in the original series-production Granturas, so it is now appropriate to survey the life of the car so far. In rather less than five years, approximately 500 cars were sold with the Wilkinson-designed trailing arm/torsion bar chassis, which changed very little during that time. After a time, incidentally, it had become known that the suspension and ride was almost insufferably hard, and it is also worth noting that the ground clearance was somewhat limited (though this altered very little on undulating roads due to the hard suspension). Even when the cars were new and correctly set up, there was some slight degree of 'rear-wheel steering' inherent in the system, due to the rubber bushes linking the trailing arms to the wheels, and this tended to worsen as wear took place.

The last of the 1962 Mark IIAs had the same basic bodyshell as the 1958 car, except for a number of detail improvements, not least of which was a growing attention to quality. It has to be

admitted that the bumpers (thin on the early Mark Is, rather more substantial on later cars) were little more than decorative appendages, but at least the glass-fibre bodyshells could easily be replaced, or repaired by any competent glass-fibre shop.

In the five years, engines fitted varied from the 35-bhp side-valve Ford to a race-tuned MGA 1600 Mark II unit (which could, perhaps, produce more than 110 bhp), and the maximum speeds varied between the claimed 75 mph of those early Ford-engined cars to the 101 mph of *The Autocar's* Stage 2 Coventry Climax-engined machine tested in November 1961 and to well over 120 mph in out-and-out racing guise.

However, these early TVRs soon fell out of fashion as the 1960s progressed, and it is doubtful if many of them now remain in anything like 'as built' condition. In any case, something like two-thirds to three-quarters of all Marks I, II and IIA were supplied by TVR in kit form, and may not have been in 'as intended' condition by the time the owners had finished personalizing their product. Now, the surviving cars are interesting as early examples of a marque which was to mature and improve progressively in the years which followed.

In 1962, however, no-one at TVR was thinking much about the old models, as the works was full of preparations for a new car. The combination of Brian Hopton, John Thurner and a new chassis design was about to become obvious.

CHAPTER 3

Mark III, Vixen and others

The new chassis — 1962 to 1972

Although John Thurner had started thinking about a new chassis design for TVR as early as 1960, it was not until 1961 that enough capital could be committed to building a prototype and preparing for production, and it was not until the spring of 1962 that the first car was completed and revealed to the public. Even though the Grantura was selling better than ever (even if the company was not actually making any money), it was thought that not only did it need a new chassis — stiffer, more efficient and with a much more supple ride — but also new styling. The new chassis duly came on stream in 1962, though the new styling was never produced for it.

It was Brian Hopton's idea that an official works competition programme should be set up to support the new TVR. Hopton then went out and hired Ken Richardson, who had been at Standard-Triumph for nearly nine years, but had left abruptly soon after the influence of Leyland Motors took hold. Even though the new chassis was not ready, Richardson became TVR's first (and only, as it transpired) competition manager.

The new chassis was meant to eliminate all the basic faults of the original Grantura variety, while remaining faithful to the multi-tubular philosophy and capable of being built on simple jigging at the Hoo Hill works. Although TVR's latest owners eventually wanted the new chassis to be graced by a new glass-fibre body, they also insisted that it should be capable of fitment under a lightly modified derivative of the existing body. The only concession they made to the modernization of the Grantura's body — from Mark IIA to Mark III — was to allow for a slightly longer wheelbase under the same exterior skin. However, although this allowed a little more interior space, and particularly leg-room (the seats being slightly further back than before), the original extremely narrow doors were retained.

The most noticeable shortcomings of the 'trailing-arm' chassis, which Trevor Wilkinson had designed and was put into series production in 1958, were that its layout was not technically very efficient, it was not very stiff in torsion and its VW-style suspension gave a very hard ride. Thurner's new chassis set out to rectify all these faults. As it transpired, the new chassis-frame and suspension were even more versatile than had been intended. They remained in production for almost 10 years — from 1962 to the spring of 1972 — and formed the basis of cars with four-cylinder, V-6, in-line six-cylinder and V-8 engines, and with a range of power outputs from the 63 bhp (DIN) of the Spitfire-engined 1300 to the 271-bhp (gross) engine fitted to some Griffiths and Tuscan V8s. From model to model, the changes were minimal — here and there a tube or a mounting bracket would be moved, or modified, to allow a different engine, gearbox, or final-drive unit to be installed.

The new chassis retained the multi-tubular layout, including the four-tube backbone wrapping around the drive train, but it was laid out in a much more stress-efficient and logical manner. Further, the VW-style trailing-link suspension system was discarded completely and replaced by front and rear double-wishbone layouts allied to coil springs — systems, incidentally, still used by many British and European 'Supercars' to this day. Before going on to describe the various TVR models which evolved around this new frame, it is necessary to describe the frame in some detail.

As I have already said, the basic wheelbase of the 1962 chassis-

The Grantura Mark III's chassis-frame, designed for TVR by John Thurner, was much more rigid than the trailing-arm-suspension chassis which it replaced in 1962. Not only was it more scientifically designed, with a better and more logical attitude to triangulation, but it was much more solid in resistance to bending and to torsional forces. This picture is taken from the rear corner, showing the very sturdy build-up of tubes around the final-drive mountings and the pick-up points for the wishbone rear suspension. Also evident are the forward and rear shut faces for the doors, the tubular outriggers to protect the passengers and the moulded-in glass-fibre floor. *(John Bailie)*

frame was 7 ft 1.5 in — 1.5 inches more than that of the obsolete trailing-link frame, and although there were no mechanical constraints except those connected with the existing bodyshell, the front and rear tracks were the same as before.

The design was arranged to make the most of the new wishbone systems, which came first, and the rest of the layout followed from this. At the front, Triumph Herald/Vitesse vertical links and lower wishbones were used, while the upper wishbone was tubular and special to TVR. Special coil spring/damper units, Triumph-type rack-and-pinion steering gear and an anti-roll bar completed a compact and thoroughly modern layout, which was allied to Triumph-type 10.75-inch Girling disc brakes.

At the rear, there was a special light-alloy vertical link by TVR, allied to wide-based tubular upper and lower wishbones. Due to the fact that the drive-shaft had to thread its way out from the chassis-mounted differential unit to the hubs, the combined coil

26

spring/damper unit had to be offset, was pivotted from the bottom of the vertical link and was behind the line of the drive-shafts. There was no anti-roll bar at the rear.

Although the frame was built up principally from 16-gauge 1.5-inch diameter steel tube, like the superseded frame, it was completely different. The obsolete design's principal drawback had been that although there was a straight and continuous run of the lower backbone tubes from front to rear, the engine bay top tube had been stopped abruptly at the bulkhead, welded to a vertical tube, and another much lower tube had then linked this vertical post to the rear suspension mountings; not only was the frame torsionally weak across the cockpit, but the bending strength, too, had been limited.

The new frame was considerably more sturdy, with tubes running smoothly and consistently (if not absolutely in a straight line) from front to rear. Substantial cages supported the front and rear suspension mountings, and there was a considerable degree of tubular triangulation in most sections. As before, there were substantial outriggers filling in the space between the front and rear wheels, along with vertical sheet-steel panels forming supports for the door cut-outs and shut faces. Although it was by no means a theoretically ideal spaceframe (not even Colin Chapman of Lotus — the acknowledged expert in these matters — could provide such a layout for a two-seater road car with large doors and adequate provision for occupants and the engine) it was a thoroughly practical layout requiring little capital expenditure on tooling, but one which TVR could make in considerable numbers. In practical terms, the only disadvantage of the new layout was that it meant that there was now a very wide and bulky gearbox tunnel running through the cockpit, something which was to be a characteristic of this range of TVRs for the next 10 years.

Externally, there was virtually no indication of the radically new and improved chassis design, for the wheels, tyres and general body lines were unchanged. Even under the bonnet, things were not dramatically different, except that the upper longitudinal chassis rails were somewhat lower than before. The only apparent penalty of the new frame was that it was between 15 and 20 lb heavier than the one it replaced, but all the extra weight had gone into making the chassis more rigid and versatile.

A 1962 Mark III rolling chassis, with its B-Series MG engine and transmission already installed. Just visible at the rear are the combined coil-spring/damper suspension units and the extra telescopic damper which was mounted ahead of the drive-shafts and upper wishbones. *(John Bailie)*

The most important feature of the new chassis design adopted for the Grantura Mark III of 1962 was the use of coil-spring independent suspension. Geometry at front and rear was by double wishbones, and the combined coil-spring/damper units pivotted from lugs on the main cross-member. The engine is a 1,622-cc MGA 1600 Mark II unit and rack-and-pinion steering had been standardized. In all respects, the chassis-frame was more sturdy, more advanced and more 'sporting' than that of its ancestors. *(Autocar)*

To go with the new frame, incidentally, there was a larger fuel tank of 10 instead of 8¾ gallons capacity — still mounted in the tail, behind the final-drive unit.

In the 10 years which followed, very few major changes were made to the design. The wheelbase was increased by 4.5 inches — from 7 ft 1.5 in to 7 ft 6 in — in 1967 for the Tuscan V8 SE and in 1968 for the Vixen S2, after which the shorter-wheelbase derivative disappeared completely, and over the years there was a marginal increase in quoted track dimensions, and light-alloy wheels came to displace the steel or centre-lock wires which were normal wear at first.

All in all, 13 different TVR models were marketed in the next 10 years on this one basic chassis design, six with the original 7-ft 1.5-in wheelbase, and seven with the 7-ft 6-in wheelbase. It would be possible, but confusing, to describe each and every one in the sequence in which they were announced, lived and died away, so now I intend to split my survey into two sections. A complete family tree of TVR models is to be found in Appendix A, showing that there were seven models in this chassis series with four-cylinder engines, and six with six-cylinder or eight-cylinder power.

The rest of this chapter, therefore, is devoted to analyzing the four-cylinder models, all of which (with one exception) followed on in sequence from a previous model, without overlap. The exception was the Triumph Spitfire-engined 1300, which came towards the end of the run of this chassis and was built at the same time as the last of the Vixen S3s and the S4s.

The Grantura Mark III and Mark III 1800

This was the original model in the 'new chassis' series, the car conceived by John Thurner for his new managing director, and the one intended to take over, directly, from the existing Grantura Mark IIA, which used the VW-style trailing-link chassis. Although it was originally revealed to the press in April 1962 (and put on show at the New York Auto Show of that month) and *The Motor* carried a full technical analysis in August, the old-type Grantura Mark IIA remained in production until the autumn, and the TVR factory was really not ready to build Mark IIIs until September/October. In the meantime, the slightly restyled bonnet, with relocated air-inlet grille, and indicators now mounted at each side of it, had been fitted to the last of the Mark IIA cars as well, thus helping to confuse historians and those

shopping for a TVR in latter years.

This explains why the cars raced at Sebring looked like Mark IIIs, but were Mark IIAs, something always difficult to understand when the complexities of sporting homologation are considered. I will return to the sad story of the 1962 works competition effort a little later in this chapter.

The major decision regarding the new Grantura Mark III was not just that it should have the new chassis, but that the MGA four-cylinder engine and gearbox should be standardized. Although it seems that a few cars were built with what I can only assume were existing stocks of Ford 109E 1,340-cc and Coventry Climax FWE 1,216-cc engines (and their appropriate gearboxes), the time of providing the customer with a large choice of engines was now past. *The Autocar* mentioned the options when they described the car in April 1962, but *The Motor's* more comprehensive analysis mentioned no option other than that of a tune-up kit centred around the HRG cross-flow light-alloy cylinder-head. No records of this transition period exist today, but I doubt if more than a handful of Ford or Coventry Climax-engined cars were built.

Compared with the original Grantura, there had been many detail changes in the styling of the Grantura Mark III of 1962-4. Notable in this shot are the rear wing extension, which had been introduced for the Mark II, the flares above the rear wheelarches, which had come along at the same time, and the reprofiling around the rear number-plate area, which was phased-in during the autumn of 1963. This car was one of the first to have the 1,798-cc MGB engine. The luggage grid was not standard. *(Autocar)*

One of three Grantura Mark IIIs built for the Ken Richardson-directed attack on the Le Mans race in 1962. Only one car actually started the race, but it retired within minutes due to the chronic overheating of its race-tuned MGA engine, in spite of the fact that three extra air-intakes (said to have been inspired by those of the Ferrari GTO) had been let into the bonnet above the normal Mark III radiator air intake. This picture was taken somewhat later, when the car had been sold to a private owner and was wearing road tyres. *(John Bailie)*

It should be noted, however, that production of the MGA sports car ran out in the summer of 1962, before the Grantura Mark III was properly in production, and it was replaced by the MGB. In practical terms, for TVR, this meant that supplies of the 86-bhp 1,622-cc engine from BMC dried up almost at once, though they were not forced to make the changeover to 1,798-cc MGB engines until the early-autumn of 1963. When this happened, there was no increase in weight, or bulk, but the power available, in standard form, was increased from 86 bhp (net) to 95 bhp (net) with a similar improvement in the torque, from 97 lb ft to 110 lb ft.

The normal MG gearbox was supplied, and once overdrive became available on MGBs (from the beginning of 1963) that option was also applied to the Grantura Mark III. As on earlier Granturas, a B-series BMC differential and final-drive assembly was provided in a special TVR light-alloy casing; various ratios were available, to choice. As with the earlier Granturas, there was no separate outside access to the luggage space, and the spare wheel had to be extracted by lifting it out of a recess behind the rear suspension, through the passenger compartment.

Officially, this car was only to be supplied as a kit, so that the customer could avoid paying Purchase Tax (in Britain, that is), though it seems certain that some completely built-up cars were supplied.

In the meantime, however, important personal and commercial events had evolved at Blackpool. In April 1962, sickened by the constant changes in policy and by what he considered to be reckless over-expansion and financial incompetence, Trevor Wilkinson left the company which he had founded. 'His' company, incidentally, had become TVR Cars Ltd following the Aitchison-Hopton takeover, and it was now well on the way to a financial crisis. High living by the directors, and far too much money spent on a competition programme, not to mention the cost of setting up for the new chassis design, all bore down heavily on the concern. Even though the Mark III was proudly displayed at the Earls Court Motor Show in October 1962, the company was in desperate trouble, and before the end of the month it had closed down altogether.

The Grantura Mark III, therefore, eventually struggled into hand-to-mouth production, basically by employees of Grantura Engineering (which had not collapsed). Messrs Hopton and Aitchison disappeared as rapidly as they had arrived on the scene, Ken Richardson's one-season job (and the competition programme) evaporated and it was left to Bernard Williams and Stan Kilcoyne to pick up the pieces. Before long, too, John Thurner left Blackpool, and returned to Rolls-Royce.

The development which saved Grantura Engineering — for a time at least — was the birth and development of the V-8-engined Griffith, but consideration of this car belongs to the next chapter. In the meantime, the Mark III went on sale, with an extra telescopic damper to each rear suspension (ahead of the wishbones, effectively balancing the spring/damper unit which was already behind the line of the drive-shafts).

In the autumn of 1963, the 1,798-cc MGB engine was standardized, minor changes were made to the shape of the tail and the location of the rear numberplate, the front upper

Because of the glass-fibre construction, it was easy for TVR owners to design and effect their own modifications, such as this opening stowage lid on an early Mark II . . . *(John Bailie)*

At the same time, the layout of the rear was changed so that the spare wheel was no longer tucked down behind the rear suspension. On the 1800S and subsequent models it was mounted on the flat rear floor of the bodyshell, immediately above the final-drive unit, inside the bodyshell, and neatly covered.

To standardize production facilities, this Manx-tail body style was adopted for the MGB-engined TVRs, which thereupon became 1800S models. S for what? Who knows? S for Short, S for Stubby, S for Sporting? Does it matter now?

The first 1800S models were built, in the summer of 1964, at a time when the Hoo Hill works was almost completely concerned with building a flood of Griffiths, purely for sale in North America. It was the combination of Griffith problems, financial naivety and sheer commercial inexperience which eventually conspired to bring another builder of TVRs to bankruptcy. The smooth and exciting Trident project certainly didn't help. The

. . . which hinged down to reveal the spare wheel, now relatively easy to extract if needed. One wonders why TVR production cars were never treated to this fitting? *(John Bailie)*

wishbone pivots were repositioned to improve the geometry, the radiator header tank was positioned above the left-side front wheelarch and the layout of the instruments was revised. At this time, incidentally, a Mark III cost £872 (basic), or £1,054 with British Purchase Tax.

Before the Mark III was displaced by the 1800S, about 90 cars were built, many of them being exported.

The Grantura 1800S

For the 1964 New York Auto Show, Grantura Engineering had built restyled Griffith models, having reshaped tails, in which the now-familiar 'Manx-tail' shape was prominent, along with a larger and sleeker rear window. (This window, incidentally, remained unchanged from this time until the last of the 3000Ms was built at the end of 1979.) Tail-lights and indicators, instead of being standard round Lucas units, gave place to the three-sector Ford Cortina Mark I (1962-6) combined tail/indicator/stoplights.

sum total of this was that Arnold Burton, who had been a major shareholder of the companies since the beginning of the 1960s, refused to fund any more losses. Major Timothy Knott, who had been Grantura's managing director for just one year, was pushed out, Bernard Williams pulled out, but kept a controlling interest in a business called Grantura Plastics (which had been set up in 1963 to supply bodyshells to Grantura Engineering — I *said* this was a complex little story!) and Grantura Engineering closed down.

I am now nearly at the end of relating corporate upheavals which afflicated the TVR motor car in its early years. Martin Lilley, who ran the Barnet Motor Co Ltd and had become a TVR dealer in the spring of 1965, was the son of Arthur Lilley, who bought some Grantura Engineering shares just before the crash. Following the close-down, Arthur Lilley made an offer for all the assets, in November 1965, which was accepted. TVR Engineering Ltd, their new company, was founded on November 30, 1965 and before the end of the year the TVR marque was back in business.

At this point, I am happy to say, I am able to start quoting very accurate production quantities, dates and Chassis Numbers, as all the TVR Engineering records have been preserved and were made available to me in preparing this book. Therefore, I am able to say that, whereas there were *approximately* 90 1800S cars built by Grantura Engineering, there were *exactly* 38 built in 1966 by TVR Engineering.

To get the Hoo Hill works back into action, Martin Lilley, appointed managing director of TVR (his father, Arthur Lilley, became chairman), concentrated on building existing models during 1966; new models would have to wait until something approaching financial stability had been achieved. The first TVR to be completed under the aegis of TVR Engineering was a Grantura 1800S, early in February 1966. Of the 38 cars built between February and September, seven had right-hand drive and most had the 4.3:1 final-drive ratio, though a few had the 3.9:1 ratio.

In July 1966, however, after the first 26 Lilley-type 1800S cars had been built, the first of a new derivative — the 'Mark IV' 1800S — was built. Chassis Numbers between 18/027 and 18/044 were intermingled, but thereafter the 'Mark IV's took over completely.

The Grantura 'Mark IV' 1800S

This car was, quite simply, a refined and improved version of the 1800S. The first was built in July 1966 and the last of all in October 1967, at which point it was displaced by the first of the Vixen family. Altogether, 78 cars were built, of which 40 had right-hand drive and 38 left-hand drive.

It was Martin Lilley's policy to upgrade TVR quality considerably, so the difference between the 1800S and the 'Mark IV' 1800S was confined to trim, furnishing and some mechanical improvements. Although *The Motor,* at the time, assured us that the 4.3:1 axle ratio had been standardized, quite a number were built with the 3.9:1 ratio. Very few, incidentally, had disc wheels. The engine/gearbox assembly had been moved forward very slightly, and compared with the 1800S the spring-and-damper settings had been revised to provide a more supple ride, while top *and* bottom wishbones were fabricated by TVR. The most obvious trim change was to the facia, where instruments and controls were now housed on a polished wooden panel. Hidden away was the heater from the MGB (with Rover P5 fresh-air outlets at each end of the facia) and there was a headlamp flasher and self-cancelling indicators.

It is interesting, though perhaps not significant today, that the price of the Grantura rocketed during 1966, from £750 to £998 for the kit. *The Motor's* December 1966 road-test 1800S cost £1,272 in all, for the heater was listed as an extra at more than £16 and the £40 close-ratio gear option was also fitted.

The Vixen S1

The last 1800S Chassis Number was 18/116 and the first of a new series of cars, the Vixens, followed on immediately — VX/117. Although the Vixen was virtually a Grantura 1800S with an engine transplant, it signalled further advance to stability by the Lilley family, and it sold in greater numbers than the 1800S; between October 1967 and October 1968, 117 Vixen S1s were built and sold.

The transplant was that a Ford Cortina GT crossflow engine of 1,599 cc, with a peak power of 88 bhp (net), mated to its own four-speed all-synchromesh Ford gearbox, took the place of the MGB engine and transmission. The good news for TVR was that the Ford installation was lighter and cheaper than the BMC power train, but the bad news for the customer was that the Vixen was marginally less powerful and there was no overdrive option, although the gearbox, at least, now had synchromesh on all forward gears. Like the last of the 1800S models the Vixen had a large, 15-gallon, fuel tank.

It was to launch the Vixen, incidentally, that TVR first made an appearance at the prestigious Earls Court Motor Show. At the beginning of the year, TVR Engineering had taken a stand at the Racing Car Show, and had decided that this really was not their type of scene any more.

Apart from the fact that the Vixen had a noticeably different exhaust note due to the use of the high-revving Ford engine, it could also be recognized by the fitment of the new wide and shallow air intake in the centre of the glass-fibre bonnet panel, which fed cool air direct to the air cleaner above the Ford engine's downdraught twin-choke Weber carburettor.

(Note: In spite of the fact that Vixen = Ford-power, a very few of the early cars were equipped with the MGB engine and gearbox!)

The Vixen S2

In October 1968, the Vixen S2 took over from the S1, and was a much more practical machine. Mechanically it was virtually unchanged, but it benefitted from the use of the longer-wheelbase (7-ft 6-in) chassis first developed for the Tuscan V8 SE (see

For the Grantura Mark III, the standard engine was the MG unit. Early examples had the 1,622-cc MGA engine, but from the autumn of 1963 the 1,798-cc MGB unit was standardized. Here is the MGB engine, neatly installed into the engine bay of a 1964-model Mark III, with the radiator header tank fixed to the wheelarch on the left side of the engine bay. The large-diameter trunking leads from the nose of the car to the heater installation — it might have looked efficient, but it wasn't! Note the neat and simple cooling vents from the engine bay to the outside world, positioned behind the front wheel cutouts. *(Autocar)*

Compare this side view of the Manx-tail Vixen Series 1 with that of a Mark I Grantura, and the differences which continued to be made to the body style become obvious. The major change from Grantura Mark III to 1800S came during 1964 and involved the reshaping of the tail and rear window. The tiny doors, however, had still not been enlarged, so entry and exit from the passenger compartment was still not very easy. *(John Bailie)*

air intake had been discarded and replaced by a long slim bulge, made necessary to clear some engine 'hang-on' equipment, and cars built from the spring of 1969 were given two new depressed-section air intakes, one at each side of the TVR bonnet badge, above and behind the main radiator air intake.

Unseen, but very significant, was the fact that the glass-fibre bodyshell was no longer moulded to the multi-tube chassis-frame during manufacture, but was bolted to it. This meant that the entire shell could be lifted off the chassis if required — something very valuable at the time, when crash repairs had to be considered, and these days, when the question of maintenance and restoration has to be considered. Henceforth, all TVR bodyshells would be bolt-on, rather than moulded units.

It is also worth noting that it was during this period that the TVR marque finally achieved stability, TVR Engineering became profitable and steady expansion of production began.

The Vixen S3

The Series 2 Vixen had been a very popular model, but it was replaced in the autumn of 1970 by the Vixen Series 3, at a time when the move from the Hoo Hill works to the Bristol Avenue factory where TVR production is now concentrated, was in progress. In the meantime, the last of the V-8-engined Tuscans had been built, the (British Ford) V-6-engined Tuscan had arrived as a 'sister' car to the Vixens, and the short series of wide-bodied Tuscan V8s had also been constructed. All these cars are covered in Chapter 4.

Visually, the Vixen Series 3 model was virtually unchanged, except that the cast-alloy road wheels introduced on the Tuscan V6 were standardized and the front wing vents (behind the front wheels) were now of a more delicately detailed type, and actually were 'Aeroflow' outlet grilles from the rear quarters of the Ford Mark IV Zephyr/Zodiac saloons.

The mechanical improvements were that the 1,599-cc Ford engine was now of the rather lustier 86 bhp (DIN) Ford Capri 1600GT variety, along with that car's gearbox, but — as before — no overdrive was available.

The Series 3 was built from October 1970 to April 1972 and the last Vixen Series 3 was also the very last chassis of the 1962-72 type to be built. A total of 168 cars were built, 50 in 1970, 97 in 1971 and 21 in 1972.

Chapter 4), where the extra wheelbase was meant to allow larger doors to be fitted, and for access to and egress from the passenger compartment to be improved.

No more than three cars a week had been built in 1967, but this rose to more than four a week in 1968 and continued to rise as more people warmed to the modern TVR manufacturing philosophy. The Series 2 Vixen, of which 438 cars would be built in almost exactly two years, carried that improvement a stage further. TVR Engineering claimed no fewer than 75 detail improvements over the Series 1 model, but it was the longer wheelbase and the visual retouching which took most attention.

Apart from the longer wheelbase, which made the larger doors so obvious, there were the latest wrap-around Cortina Mark II tail/indicator lamps (instead of the circular Cortina Mark I lamps), a modified bonnet moulding, in which the forward-facing

The Vixen S4

The Series 4 Vixen was one of the 'interim' TVRs built in 1972-3 and was effectively a Vixen Series 3 bodyshell, equipment and power train, allied to the M-type chassis which is described fully in Chapter 5. In total, 23 cars were built — 22 in 1972, and just one in 1973. The Vixen series was then discontinued and replaced by the 1600M model.

The 1300

In the entire life of the Mark III chassis-frame, only one four-cylinder model was not a Grantura or a Vixen, and this was the 1300. It was a short-lived and, frankly, unsuccessful car, powered by a 1,296-cc Triumph Spitfire engine and that car's all-synchromesh gearbox and it looked exactly like the Series 3 Vixen and Tuscan V6 models which were current at the time. The car weighed 1,625 lb — about 60 lb more than the Spitfire itself — and it had considerably more frontal area. Although a TVR 1300 was never road-tested, it may be assumed that its maximum speed was between 90 and 95 mph, and that the acceleration would be similar to that of the Spitfire, which recorded 0-60mph in 16

The badge tells us that this was a Vixen, and the number-plate denotes a car registered between August 1968 and August 1969, while the use of those unmistakable 'Ban the Bomb' tail-lamp clusters from the Ford Cortina Mark I finally clinch the identification — this is a Series I Vixen. *(John Bailie)*

This Series I Vixen is posed at Mallory Park circuit. It is visually non-standard in that the Tuscan V6/Vixen Series 2 type of bonnet has been fitted, the derivative being recognized by the two cold-air intakes in the bonnet, roughly as far back as the centre line of the front wheels. Many TVRs have been modernized in this way, often due to an accident having necessitated a new section to the body. *(John Bailie)*

seconds and a standing quarter-mile in 20.6 seconds in *Autocar's* hands.

It was not a success, not only because it was not fast enough (probably *every* production TVR except the Ford 100E and 105E-powered examples was quicker), but also because it was not particularly cheap. The basic price of a 1300 in 1971 was £1,245, which was only £50 cheaper than that of the Vixen Series 3.

Only nine 1300s of the original type were sold, along with five having the M-type chassis (as with the Vixen Series 4 model), while one final 1300 should really have been called a 1300M, as it had the M-type bodyshell as well.

The 1962 works competition programme

As mentioned earlier in this chapter, the Aitchison-Hopton regime instituted a works competition programme in 1962, which ended up by costing TVR Cars Ltd a great deal of money and

The neat engine bay installation of the Cortina GT 1,599-cc engine in the Vixen Series 2, showing the unaltered circular Ford air-cleaner, the trunking to the heater and yet another minor variation on the radiator filler cap position. As ever, access for maintenance was superb. Incidentally, the front wing vents are of an interim type, soon ditched in favour of the Ford Mark IV aeroflow vents. *(Autocar)*

One consequence of the restyling of the tail, in 1964, to the 'Manx-tail' layout was that the spare wheel henceforth had to be stored under a cover in the stowage space behind the seats. This particular car is a Vixen Series 2, and it demonstrates that this spare wheel position had a devastating effect on the amount of space which could be used for luggage. *(Autocar)*

achieved nothing.

To run the programme, Brian Hopton hired Ken Richardson as TVR's competition manager. Richardson had a great deal of experience in racing and rallying road-going sports cars, as he had set up Standard-Triumph's competitions programme in 1954 and had led his department for seven years, during which the Triumph TRs and the prototype twin-cam TR3S and TRS models had raced with some success at Le Mans. However, the facilities available to him at Standard-Triumph were much more lavish than they were to be at Blackpool. Richardson, however, was 'between jobs' — having left Standard-Triumph in the late-summer of 1961 — and was anxious to get back into the sporting scene again.

TVR's first foray, in an effort carried out in great haste, was to send a team of three Grantura Mark IIAs to the Sebring 12-hour race. A measure of the rush was that Ken Richardson took up his job in January 1962, the cars left for Florida by sea in February, and the race itself was in March.

The three cars were fitted with the optional lightweight bodyshells and right-hand drive, though they had the new Mark III bonnets and air intakes. Special equipment fitted to the race-prepared 1,588-cc MGA engines included the cross-flow, light-alloy, HRG cylinder-head and twin horizontal dual-choke Weber carburettors. There was no success at Sebring, which could surely only have been expected, for one car broke its final-drive, one suffered engine failure after four hours and the third (driven by Mark Donohue and Gerry Sagerman) finished well back after crashing and having to have new steering parts fitted.

The next outing was the International Tulip Rally, which started and finished at Noordwijk-an-Zee, on the Dutch coast, and ran as far south as Monte Carlo for an overnight halt. There were three works entries — Arnold Burton and Coventry haulage contractor Stan Pateman in their own Grantura Mark IIs, teamed up with Anne Hall/Valerie Domleo in a factory-prepared Grantura Mark IIA. The registration number of Anne's car was 880 ABM, which adds considerably to the mystery as this is a Bedfordshire, not a Lancashire, numberplate! Like the Sebring car, this had the new Mark III type of bonnet panel, and it was also fitted with the optional engine parts and the all-synchromesh ZF gearbox.

At one stage in the rally, TVR cars were in the first three positions in their class, but the ladies' car became stuck in third gear for many hours, then Anne Hall put it off the road and retired it. Two Porsche Super 90s then dominated the class, and Arnold Burton took third place behind them.

None of the Sebring race cars returned to Britain, and for the Le Mans 24-hour race, three brand new Mark IIIs were prepared. Incidentally, although production had not properly begun, Brian Hopton was determined to use the Mark IIIs, even though he could not yet deliver replicas, and Richardson was reputedly delighted as the handling with the new chassis was much superior to that of the Mark IIAs used at Sebring. Only one firm entry had been granted, along with one reserve place, so at best only two of the three cars could hope to start.

In the event, only the one car — YFR 751, to be driven by Peter Bolton and Ninian Sanderson — took the start, as not enough other cars dropped out in the practice sessions for the reserve

A padded dash panel was adopted for the Series 2 Vixen, and the switchgear was modified yet again. It was an area which always seemed to be the subject of change, or 'improvement', at TVR — a process which continued throughout the 1970s. *(Autocar)*

(YFR 752, to have been driven by Rob Slotemaker and Ted Lund) to qualify. In practice, both cars were sorely troubled with engine overheating, which seemed to occur whenever they slowed down considerably after flat-out speeds along the Mulsanne straight. Cooling problems were suspected, but no obvious solution was to hand, and the race car started without modifications.

The race itself was a disaster. Peter Bolton took the first driving stint, but the engine rapidly boiled its water away, and after only three laps — about 15 minutes of racing — the car stood at its pit, steaming away, the engine ruined.

It was almost the same story at the Tourist Trophy race, held at Goodwood, in August. Three Mark IIIs (the same three cars which had been prepared for Le Mans) were entered, three practised, and there was more engine overheating trouble during practice. Rob Slotemaker's car never left the marshalling area before the start, which left Peter Bolton and Keith Ballisat to take up the running.

Bolton's car blew a cylinder-head gasket soon after the start, but

The Vixen Series 3 saw one more step along the way towards a smoother and more sophisticated TVR — a process gradually and persistently carried out by Martin Lilley in the late-1960s and early-1970s. From this low viewpoint, the recognition points which distinguish a Series 3 from the displaced Series 2 are the more delicately detailed under-bonnet outlet grilles (from the Aeroflow vents of a Ford Zodiac Mark IV), the optional cast-alloy road wheels and the slightly wrapped-round Ford Cortina Mark 2 tail-lamp clusters. However, much the most important change was to the wheelbase, which went up from 7 ft 1.5 in to 7 ft 6 in at the start of the Series 3 production. The extra 4.5 inches went into the lengthening of the doors, which at last were of a sensible size. *(TVR)*

somehow, miraculously, Keith Ballisat's machine — to his great delight — made it to the finish, 11th overall, and beaten only by Coventry Climax-engined Lotus Elites, which had engines smaller than its own.

That, however, was the end of TVR's works efforts, for TVR Cars Ltd descended into bankruptcy in October, Grantura Engineering took up the challenge in a much more restricted way, and no money was available for works competition activities.

Meanwhile, whereas the four-cylinder-engined cars made up the bread-and-butter of TVR's activities, particularly towards the end of the 1960s and the early-1970s, when production was being pushed up from four cars a week to five, from five to six, and — by 1971 — to seven or even eight, it was the six-cylinder and eight-cylinder TVRs which brought much of the glamour, excitement and even notoriety to the Blackpool concern. Although these were all closely related to the more numerous four-cylinder models, they need a separate study, and this now follows.

CHAPTER 4

Griffith, Tuscan and 2500

Mainly for export — 1963 to 1972

By 1963, the companies building TVRs had already gone through three lots of capital, and the latest concern to take on the challenge — Grantura Engineering — were operating on a very hand-to-mouth basis. There had always been a great deal of trouble in establishing profitability, even with the relatively simple four-cylinder-engined TVRs. Nevertheless, Grantura Engineering were then tempted towards more costly and exciting things when Jack Griffith, an American motor trader who owned a Mark III Grantura, installed a mighty 4.7-litre Ford V-8 engine into that car and observed the shattering results.

The story began in 1962, when Gerry Sagerman and Mark Donohue, both of whom had driven a works TVR at Sebring for Ken Richardson, were having their own cars maintained at Griffith's workshops in North America. Donohue's car was a Ford V-8-engined AC Cobra and Sagerman's was a 1962 TVR Grantura. One day, just for fun (or so the story goes), mechanics dropped the engine from Donohue's Cobra into the engine bay of Sagerman's TVR, to see if it would fit.

It wouldn't, quite, but Jack Griffith saw the unauthorized 'transplant', was inspired by the very idea of it, and determined to do the job properly. He then carried out a complete and operational 4.7-litre installation into a Grantura Mark III, and although there were handling and braking problems to be overcome, he became obsessed with the project and approached TVR on the subject. The result was that TVR's North American distributor, Dick Monnich, brought the prototype over to Blackpool, Arnold Burton put money into Grantura Engineering to finance the project, and the first deliveries began later that year. Although we must properly call the car a TVR Griffith,

Jack Griffith secured the right to market the car in North America, and merely called it a Griffith as he reasoned — quite correctly — that it had been his idea! The car made its public bow at the Boston Motor Show, in Massachusetts, when it was placarded as a Griffith 200.

This, therefore, was the first of several models designed, if not specifically for North America, then with an eye to exporting most of production to that continent. The Griffiths were followed by the Tuscan V8s, the V8s then spawned off (British Ford) V6 models, and eventually there was also to be a straight-six (Triumph-powered) car which was more practical and more successful than any of the others.

Although one car led to another, it was not always an easy or logical progression, so I propose to analyze and describe each model on its own, and relate it to others in the same general family.

The Griffith 200 and 400 models

For British readers of this book, the first thing to make clear is that the vast majority of all the Griffiths were exported to the United States, and I would be very surprised if more than a handful of V-8-engined TVRs are still in Britain.

Compared with the chassis and suspension of the Grantura Mark III, on which the US-built prototype had been developed, there are several significant differences. The basic chassis-frame was not changed — tube diameters were not increased, neither was the wall thickness of the tubes — but suspension pick-up points were strengthened. In place of the Grantura Mark III's secondary damper to each side of the rear suspension, a second

Warren Allport, of *Autocar,* peering over the scuttle of the 1965 Griffith 400 which the magazine tried briefly at the beginning of 1965. Apart from the large and prominent bulge in the bonnet moulding, there was virtually no other indication that this car had a V-8 Ford engine. *(Autocar)*

combined coil spring/damper unit was attached. Spring and damper settings were revised, not only because of this, but to take account of the extra weight of the 4.7-litre V-8 engine mounted up front. Surprisingly enough, the original 200-Series Griffiths retained the BMC B-Series final-drives, and the drive-shafts to match, which seemed to cope remarkably well in spite of the huge over-stressing which they received.

The visual changes were obvious. At the front there was a sizable bonnet bulge, made necessary to clear the air-cleaner of the large American engine, and at the rear there were twin tail-pipes to the new exhaust system, which obviously had been necessary. Fatter-section (185) radial-ply tyres were specified, and the 72-spoke wire wheels had 5-in rim widths.

There were two degrees of engine tune — rated at 195 bhp (gross) and 271 bhp (gross). The 195-bhp engine gave birth to the car's '200' title, it is thought, and this was a real mass-production unit to be found in several other American Fords of the day and in the AC Cobra (or AC 289 as it would also, eventually, be named).

The 271-bhp engine was a truly sporting unit, available at extra cost on several such cars, and one also destined to be the most powerful unit offered on the Ford Mustang of 1964.

Subsequent experience suggests that the engine outputs equated to something like 150 bhp and 220 bhp (net) respectively, which doesn't sound as exceptional, but the fact still remains that the performance of a Griffith was quite phenomenal by any standards. Certainly, in straight-line performance, if not in ultimate road behaviour, the car was quite good enough to severely embarrass an E-type Jaguar and many V-12-engined Ferraris!

When Jack Griffith did the deal with Grantura Engineering, not only was he in a great hurry to get some cars delivered and on sale, but he insisted that they should be supplied to him without engines and gearboxes (the gearboxes, by the way, were the same type as those used in the Cobra), so that he could have them fitted in his own workshops on the East Coast of the United States.

It is only fair to say that Grantura Engineering had neither the capital, the time, nor the resources, properly to cope with the technical and commercial demands of Jack Griffith, and the result was that production got under way slowly, and the original cars were by no means properly developed. The main problem was that the engines were often found to overheat — which is hardly surprising when the small size of the bonnet air intake (the same as that for the Grantura Mark III) is considered.

No-one can now say how many of the original Griffith 200s were built, but what is certain is that the machine which followed — the Griffith 400 — was a better all-round car. Firstly, and most obviously, it was the original TVR to be treated to a cut-off 'Manx' tail, complete with circular Ford Cortina Mark I tail-lamp/indicator units, and the first of these cars was built in the early spring of 1964. In addition, the Griffith 400s were also

Very few Griffith 200s — those with the Grantura Mark III tail treatment — were ever built. This was one of them, without its engine and transmission, about to leave for the construction to be completed in the United States. The company title on the wall was already obsolete, for the picture was taken in 1963 and TVR Cars Ltd had descended into bankruptcy in 1962. (John Bailie)

Typical of a crowded engine bay for any of the Ford V-8-engined TVRs was this Tuscan V8 of 1967. The tubular chassis-frame needed to be modified to accept the great width of the 4.7-litre engine, but the bodyshell was wide enough, and the only major body change needed was to incorporate a hump in the bonnet moulding to give clearance to the air-cleaner. *(John Bailie)*

Martin Lilley's own short-wheelbase Tuscan V8 under test by *Motor* magazine in the spring of 1967. 500ML , which has survived and is now nicely restored in the hands of a TVR Car Club member, had a 271-bhp engine and was shatteringly fast; its top speed was estimated at more than 155 mph by *Motor,* and it was able to sprint to a quarter-mile from rest in a mere 14.1 seconds. Not even an M-Series Turbo could match that. In all respects except for the bonnet bulge, a Tuscan V8 looked like a Grantura 1800S, with which it was concurrent. *(Motor)*

fitted with thermostatically controlled Kenlowe cooling fans, which — together with a much larger-capacity water radiator — helped to cure the overheating problems.

The Griffith 400s were exhibited at the New York Auto Show of April 1964 (incidentally, this was the same show at which the 4.2-litre Ford V-8-engined Sunbeam Tiger also made its debut), and soon the engineless cars were being turned out by the Blackpool factory at five a week, a rate which doubled by the end of 1964 (and sometimes approached 15 a week); this was the highest rate of TVR building ever achieved, before or since.

The 400, however, was not a properly developed car, especially the version which was fitted with the optional 271-bhp engine. The Griffiths often showed off the worst traits of cars which were not only designed and built in a great hurry, but were also assembled without due attention to quality of construction. Complaints piled up — not least from Jack Griffith to the factory — and the car's reputation began to suffer.

Until the beginning of 1965, each and every Griffith had officially been sent to North America. At the 1965 Racing Car Show, however, which was held at Olympia in January, the Griffith was made available in Britain, priced at £1,342 (basic), or £1,620 (total) for the 195-bhp model, £1,488 and £1,797, respectively, for the 271-bhp model.

In the meantime, the Anglo-US business relationship concerning Griffiths was shattered by a prolonged dock strike in the USA, which paralysed British exports to that country and ruined the finances of both Grantura Engineering and the Griffith assembly business. It was the beginning of the end for the

The facia of the short-wheelbase Tuscan V8, crowded with instruments and switchgear, was entirely different in detail from that of the Grantura 1800S, though both cars used the same type of Triumph Spitfire/GT6 steering column. (Motor)

This heavily retouched artist's impression is of the Tuscan V6 — basically a Tuscan V8 with a 3-litre British Ford engine. The side-lamps drawn in for this study were never used, but the engine bay vents and the depressed nostril air-intakes were. The long bonnet bulge was needed to clear the V6's air-cleaner. Cast-alloy wheels of this pattern were introduced specially for the Tuscan V6, and the style was later adopted by the Vixens and 2500s. *(John Bailie)*

Griffith and a major factor in the eventual demise of Grantura Engineering.

Although Grantura collapsed during 1965 (and the production of the Griffith failed with this collapse), it was not quite the end of the mighty V-8-engined car. Once the Lilley family had taken over the remains of the TVR business, and had got things going again, they put the existing models back into production. As already related in Chapter 3, the major activity in 1966 concerned the Grantura 1800S models, but the new concern, TVR Engineering, also managed to turn out 10 Griffiths. Therefore, although we can only say that *approximately* 300 Griffiths were produced by Grantura Engineering between 1963 and 1965, we can say with confidence that *exactly* 10 were assembled by the new concern.

A study of the Chassis Books show that the first of these cars was built in April 1966 and the last in January 1967. Four had right-hand drive, while six had left-hand drive. Incidentally, in spite of the fact that the car had officially been a Griffith 400 since the Manx-tail style was adopted, the Chassis Numbers of these final cars were prefixed with the number 200. . . .

Although I cannot be definite about this, it is estimated that no more than 20 Griffith models were delivered in Britain — all the rest originally went to the USA, and this is where most of the survivors undoubtedly are today.

The Tuscan V8

Mechanically, the car which took over from the Griffith *was* a Griffith, though it was renamed in an unsuccessful attempt to kill off the Griffith's bad reputation. Indeed, the new car, called a Tuscan V8 by Martin Lilley, was so nearly like the Griffith that it took up the same sequence of Chassis Numbers: the last of the Lilley-management Griffiths was 200-010 and was built in January 1967, while the very first Tuscan used 200-011 and followed on immediately.

Like the Grantura 1800S, the Tuscan V8 was treated to higher-quality fittings and had a highly-polished wooden facia panel; this, however, was quite different in detail from that fitted to the 1800S. If the car was fitted with the 'soft' 195-bhp engine it was known as a Tuscan V8, but if the optional 271-bhp engine was specified, it became a Tuscan V8 SE (Special Equipment).

Even though TVR had appointed a new USA distributor (Gerry Sagerman, who had indirectly been responsible for the birth of the Griffith in 1963), the sad story of the Griffith had destroyed the reputation of this car in that continent. Despite the name change from Griffith to TVR Tuscan V8, it was all too obvious that the two cars were basically the same. The Tuscan V8 had received some development, notably to the cooling system, but it was still by no means cheap.

In Britain, in 1967, the 195-bhp Tuscan V8 was priced at £1,967 — which was exactly the price asked by Jaguar for an open E-type — while the 271-bhp Tuscan V8 SE cost £2,364 — which was £80 *more* than that asked for the svelte 2+2 E-type Coupe. That was the nature of TVR Engineering's problem in 1967, and it showed in the sales achieved. In six months, a mere 28 Tuscan V8s were built, just four of them with right-hand drive.

In the meantime, however, Martin Lilley had been developing the basic concept, and the Tuscan V8 long-wheelbase model was the result.

The Tuscan V8 SE LWB
Even as the Tuscan V8 was being launched at the beginning of

1967, work was going ahead to produce its successor. This was significant because it was the first attempt by the new management to update and improve the Grantura chassis and body, which had originally joined together in 1962. Not only did the new car have a lengthened chassis, but it was also significantly restyled as well.

The multi-tubular chassis had its wheelbase lengthened from 7 ft 1.5 in to 7 ft 6 in and this figure was not changed again until 1980, when the long-running M-Series models were finally withdrawn. Due to the simple nature of the layout, this stretch was fairly easily arranged, and its purpose was to allow the doors to be lengthened and for more space to be built into the passenger compartment. The suspension layout and almost every mechanical fitting connected to the chassis was unchanged. The extra 4.5 inches went into lengthening the longitudinal chassis tubes, and of course a longer propeller-shaft and exhaust system were required. The lengthened chassis, incidentally, had originally been conceived for the Trident project, which is described in Chapter 9.

To match the lengthened doors, the long-wheelbase Tuscan V8

Retouched, but still representative of the Tuscan V6 model built from 1969 to 1971, which used the Manx-tail body first seen in 1964 and discontinued in 1972. The wrap-around Ford Cortina Mark II tail-lamp clusters were a feature, and the twin tail-pipes plus Tuscan V6 badging made this particular TVR quite unmistakable for another. Like all TVRs built from the 1968 model-year onwards, the Tuscan V6 had a 7-ft 6-in wheelbase. *(John Bailie)*

SE was also given the latest Ford Cortina Mark II tail-lamp/indicator assemblies (which replaced what are affectionately called the 'Ban the Bomb' style of circular assemblies from the Cortina Mark I) and a different bonnet moulding, which included a longer and more shapely central bulge (to clear the engine air-cleaner) and different air vents.

Appropriately, the Chassis Number sequence was changed for the new car, which took on the LWB prefix. They were no more successful than the original short-wheelbase Tuscan V8s however, for only 24 machines (one a rolling chassis, exhibited at the Earls Court Motor Show) were built in about a year. Half of them had right-hand drive.

This car, however, gave rise to another, even more significant, model, which was also a Tuscan V8 SE, but had a quite different bodyshell. What I propose to call the 'wide-body' Tuscan V8 LWB was announced at the 1968 New York Auto Show and carried the chassis prefix of MAL (Martin Lilley's initials — for it was Martin who was mainly responsible for the restyle). Between April 1968, when the first car was built, and August 1970, only 21 of these cars were assembled, all but two of which had left-hand drive.

It was the first time that the TVR coupe body style had been comprehensively reworked. Based on the lengthened (7-ft 6-in wheelbase) chassis and retaining the same glass as the existing models, the new body was four inches wider below the waistline and had completely new and much smoother lines around the nose and the tail. At the rear, the Mark II Cortina tail-light clusters were neatly moulded into the corners, and at the front there were new sidelamps. New bumpers completed the picture of what was a very smart new car.

Although it required new moulds and was more comprehensively equipped than any previous TVR, Martin Lilley made no attempt to fit this bodyshell to the lower-powered TVRs and, as a consequence, it was destined to become a loss making project.

It was, however, a real pointer to the future, and certainly formed the theme on which the definitive M-Series body style was based. Note, however, that the last of the 'wide-body' Tuscans was built in the summer of 1970, while the first-ever M-Series car was not completed until the autumn of 1971, and production did not begin until April 1972.

The Tuscan V6

Once the TVR marque became re-established, it was clear to Martin Lilley that there was a huge marketing gap between the 1.6-litre four-cylinder-engined Vixen and the 4.7-litre V-8-engined Tuscans. However, it was not until 1969 that the new company, TVR Engineering, was in a sufficiently healthy condition to consider another additional model. The result was the Tuscan V6, first put into production in mid-1969 and price listed (at £1,492 basic, £1,930 total, in Britain) from May 1969.

The fact that its Chassis Number sequences were prefixed by the letters LVX (as for the Vixen Series 2 and Series 3 models and effectively meaning Long Vixen) accurately denotes the Tuscan V6 as being an extension of the Vixen theme, rather than a 'tamed' version of the slow-selling Tuscan V8s. The name, in a way, was more of a misnomer than one might think at first.

By 1969, TVR Engineering had satisfactory commercial links with the Ford Motor Company (they had been trading with them since the late-1950s) and there was little difficulty in fixing up supplies of Ford Zodiac V-6 engines and gearboxes for their new car. (Note that, strictly speaking, the Tuscan did not use *Capri* 3-litre units at first, as this model was not officially announced until October 1969, several months after the Tuscan V6 went on sale). These engines, incidentally, were almost identical with those supplied by Ford to other companies like Reliant, for the Scimitar GTE, and Gilbern, for the Genie/Invader models, not forgetting TVR's main rival, Marcos.

The rolling chassis was effectively that of the Vixen Series 2, for only the one combined coil spring/rear damper was used (along with a secondary damper), though the servo-assisted brakes of the Tuscan V8 were standardized and the cast-alloy wheels had 5.5-in rim widths. Compared with the Vixen, which had 88 bhp (nett), the Tuscan V6 had 136 bhp (nett) or 128 bhp (DIN) as Ford liked to have it quoted, which represented a more-than-50 per cent increase in maximum power and torque. The gearing of the Tuscan V6 was considerably higher than that of the Vixen (its final-drive ratio was 3.31:1 at first, 3.54:1 later on, compared with 3.89:1 for the Vixen), but it was still a car which accelerated much more smartly, and it had a maximum speed of up to 125 mph.

It is also indicative of how much of a hybrid the Tuscan V6 really was that it retained the massive Salisbury 4HU differential and final-drive unit (as fitted to the V-8-engined cars), rather than used the smaller BMC or Triumph differentials favoured by the four-cylinder cars. There is a complete list of differential fittings — unit against model — at the end of Appendix B, the section covering technical specifications.

The Tuscan V6 could be recognized by its badging on the Manx tail (the widened body of the final Tuscan V8s was not used), its twin exhaust tailpipes and its distinctive exhaust note. It was an acceptable compromise in many ways, but it was not an outstandingly successful car. At a time when Vixen sales were reaching towards six cars a week, those of the Tuscan V6 never achieved even two cars a week. It was in production from mid-1969 until the end of 1971 (ie, just before the last of the 1962-72 chassis were assembled), during which a total of 101 cars were built and sold.

The main problem was that its engine was not 'de-toxed' for sale in North America, where the majority of TVR's exports were concentrated. TVR Cars of America Ltd, founded by Gerry Sagerman in 1966, were now making headway with the rehabilitation of the marque, and they needed a model with an engine which could meet the ever-tightening demands of the North American legislators. The Ford V-6 engine was not being exported to the USA (though the new Pinto engine was scheduled to go, and the existing Vixen's 'Kent' unit was also on sale there in some Ford models), and Ford had no plans to have the engine redeveloped to qualify. TVR Engineering, for their part, simply could not afford to do the job themselves.

Therefore, when the Tuscan V6 had only been on sale for about a year, work began at Blackpool on yet another derivative — one which would, above all, be aimed straight at North America; V-6 power was ditched and straight-six power was adopted. The result was the TVR 2500, the first-ever TVR model to have a straight-six-cylinder engine.

The TVR 2500

The key to the success of the new car was its engine. TVR cast around for a unit already selling in the United States, one which was also scheduled for persistent development with a view to it continuing to meet the regulations in future years. They found just such a unit at Triumph — the de-toxed 2,498-cc unit, an overhead-valve straight-six which had first been used in the TR250 of 1967 and was the engine currently powering the TR6

The British Ford V-6 3-litre engine slips neatly into the frame and engine bay which was also quite large enough to accept the rather more bulky American Ford 4.7-litre V-8. TVR cognoscenti will notice yet another derivative of the 'where shall we put the header tank' theme. Note the direct-acting vacuum servo for the brakes (ahead of the toeboard) and the battery in its habitual position to the left side of the under-bonnet space. The 3-litre engine became the mainstay of TVR cars of the 1970s; this was its first use, in 1969. *(John Bailie)*

Carb model built exclusively for North America. It was neither as powerful nor as torquey as the Ford 3-litre V-6, but it was fully certified and likely to remain so. As supplied by British Leyland (Triumph had been a part of that combine since it was founded, in 1968) the engine produced 106 bhp (net) at 4,900 rpm and came complete with a sturdy all-synchromesh gearbox and

A very exclusive (and expensive-to-build) TVR of 1968-70 was what is now known as the wide-body Tuscan V8. This car used the longer-wheelbase (7-ft 6-in chassis) and the power train of the Tuscan V8s, but was treated to an entirely different and smoother bodyshell, which Martin Lilley personally helped to style. Its nose was longer, its tail was smoother and it was four inches wider below the waistline. *(Autocar)*

One of the early 2500M models of 1972, showing off the distinctive lines of the M-Series body, clearly but not directly developed from those of the wide-body Tuscan V8s of 1968-70. Recognition points include the engine size marking, the early type of cast-alloy wheels, the Zodiac Mark IV type of engine bay cooling hole grille and the chrome bumpers. On these early cars, too, the wrap-around Cortina Mark 2 rear-lamp clusters were retained. *(John Bailie)*

optional overdrive. Also in the package, as developed by TVR, was the chassis-mounted differential and final-drive unit from the same Triumph TR6 model, one which became of supreme importance to TVR throughout the 1970s.

It all came together in the nick of time, for the Tuscan V6 was quite unsuitable for export (only seven cars were sold overseas) and the Ford Cortina/Capri 1,599-cc unit was just about to run into several development problems regarding the USA de-toxing requirements.

The TVR 2500 used the Tuscan V6/Vixen S3 rolling chassis, with Tuscan V6-width 5.5-in wheel rims, and had a smaller fuel tank — to take account of yet more evaporative-loss regulations — than the Vixen or Tuscan models. Although it was shown at the Earls Court Motor Show in October 1970, it was not quite ready to be put on sale. The first production model, Chassis Number 1745/6T (6T = six-cylinder Triumph) followed in November, and the full flood of production began at the turn of the year. It was not until April, however, that British magazines were issued with an interesting overhead picture showing the Triumph 2500 rolling chassis, alongside and in front of a complete 2500 car. The

One of the only two right-hand-drive wide-body Tuscan V8s in captivity is this extensively restored example, now owned by Robert Nosowicz, which used to be Martin Lilley's own car, and in its present (1980 photograph) state has a much-modified 289-cu in (4,727-cc) V-8 engine, special wheels and tyres and a detachable Perspex roof panel. Robert uses the car in sprints and other competitions, which explains the number on the door. *(Robert Nosowicz)*

British price was £1,475 (in kit form, without Purchase Tax) and £1,927 (complete), though these prices began to escalate before long, as Britain's 1970s inflation had now begun to worsen alarmingly.

Surprisingly, TVR and Martin Lilley were never tempted to sell the 2500 in non-US market guise with the much more powerful fuel-injected TR5 engine (which produced peak power of 150 bhp at 5,500 rpm), and the result was that the 2500, though a lively enough car, was not markedly quicker than the Vixen S3, which continued to be very popular.

The 2500 was a great success by any previous and current TVR standards. Although only eight cars were started in 1970, no fewer than 237 were assembled in 1971, compared with 97 Vixens, and production was still going ahead at full-blast when the last of the Grantura-type chassis was assembled in the spring

of 1972. Not only were a further 44 original-type 2500s built in the first few months of 1972, but a further 95 cars of the 'hybrid' type were built in 1972 with the new M-Series chassis and the old-style bodyshell, and another of these 'hybrids' was built in 1973.

It follows from these remarks that there was a considerable overlap during 1972 (and, to a lesser extent, in 1973) between the 2500, which had the old type of chassis-frame, the 'hybrid' 2500, which linked the old-style body with the M-Series frame, and the 2500M, which used the familiar drive train in the M-Series frame topped by the M-Series body style. All very confusing.

Of the 2500s, therefore, 289 were completely old-style cars and 96 were M-Series chassis/old-style body cars — making a total production of 385. Of these, at least two-thirds were exported to North America.

The last of the completely old-style 2500s was Chassis Number 2237/T, which was not quite the last of all the old-style frames,

Overhead view of Robert Nosowicz's ex-Martin Lilley wide-body Tuscan V8, showing off the large aperture in the glass-fibre roof, which is normally filled by a Perspex panel. The engine is now heavily modified and features four downdraught twin-choke Weber carburettors. *(Robert Nosowicz)*

and the last of the 'hybrids' was 2703/T, and was commissioned in May 1973.

In detailing the development of the more powerful TVRs of the 1960s and early-1970s, I have had to ignore the major business change which occurred during the period. Early in 1970, negotiations began for a new factory to be acquired at Bristol Avenue, Bispham, Blackpool, and at the end of 1970 the move was completed. It allowed plans for the 1970s to be pushed ahead — somehow, at the old Hoo Hill works, the future had always seemed to be such an ephemeral vision — and these included the design of another new chassis *and* body style. The result was the M-Series cars, where M stood for Martin. If the 1950s had been all about learning and the 1960s all about survival, the 1970s were to see TVR come to maturity.

A splendid picture originally issued by TVR in 1971, which shows off not only the relationship between the late-model Vixen-type coil-sprung chassis and the smoothed-out bodyshell used between 1969 and 1972, but also the detail of the chassis, and the way in which the de-toxed six-cylinder 2,498-cc Triumph TR6 engine and gearbox fits into the frame. The contours of the longitudinal tubes by this time were fixed by the need to clear the bulky Ford V-6 and V-8 engines. In this case, the final-drive assembly is from a Triumph TR6. The sunshine roof on the car was an optional extra, and the rear-facing bonnet air outlets were to keep the federalized engine adequately cool. *(TVR)*

CHAPTER 5

1600M, 2500M and 3000M

M for Martin — the 1970s TVRs

As far as motoring journalists were concerned, a visit to the TVR stand at the 1971 Earls Court Motor Show was a memorable experience. Not only were there two new TVR models to be seen, but the Press Day celebrations were also enlivened by the presence of two nude models cavorting around the cars. It brought TVR more publicity, of one kind or another, than they had ever expected, though I doubt if even one per cent of all the pictures which were taken ever found their way into print.

The two new cars on show were the Spitfire-engined 1300, which had been in production since August 1971, and the 2500M, which was just a prototype rushed to the show immediately after it had been built at Blackpool. That car, incidentally, carried Chassis Number 2090T; does it still survive? There was also the SM, or Zante prototype, but that's another story, covered in Chapter 8.

The 2500M's launch, in fact, was curiously muted, especially as it was to prove to be the cornerstone of TVR's prosperity in the 1970s. I well remember seeing the car, noting that it had different front and rear styling and wondering what all the fuss was about. At the time, no fuss was made of the car's most significant feature — its new chassis — perhaps because this wasn't even fitted to the show car, but was added later.

The design of an all-new chassis for the cars of the 1970s signalled to TVR watchers that the Lilley family now had long-term confidence in the marque which they had bought in 1965. They were ready to make a large investment in TVR Engineering, not only to provide a new image, but to help eradicate some of the shortcomings of the past.

By 1971, the existing TVR chassis, which had originally been used in the Grantura Mark III of 1962, had been in production for more than nine years. In that time, its wheelbase had been lengthened once, the profile of the tubes around the engine bay had been modified to take account of the various engines used over the years, and it was still a frame which was more or less assembled by hand by skilled craftsmen. Not only this, but it had always had something of a reputation for steering kick-back and other development maladies.

In the meantime, Mike Bigland, an engineer and TVR dealer from the Midlands, had built up a special Tuscan V8 for a customer incorporating many chassis modifications. After a visit to see Martin Lilley at Blackpool, Bigland got together with Martin to evolve a new chassis design incorporating some of those ideas and to form the basis for the new range of models. This soon became known as the 'M-Series' design, and as already mentioned, M stood for Martin.

Although the prototype frame was completed in the autumn of 1971, the factory was not yet ready to produce it in quantity. Existing Vixen-type frames continued to be built in large quantities for several more months after the 2500M prototype was shown at Earls Court, and the first 'off-tools' example was not built until April 1972. At that time, however, there was a simple and straightforward functional (and statistical) changeover. The last of the old-style frames was Chassis Number LVX/2239/4, and it formed the basis of a Vixen Series 3, while the first of the M-Series frames was Chassis Number 2240TM, and it became the original 2500M production car. There was no overlap and no confusion.

As with all previous TVR production cars, the new M-Series

The engine bay of the 2500M, the only TVR so far built with a straight-six-cylinder engine. This was the detoxed Triumph TR6 unit, which produced about 106 bhp. On all M-Series cars the spare wheel was carried in the nose, ahead of whatever engine was fitted and above the cooling radiator. The trunking for the heater installation was now to the near-side of the engine bay, and the bay on the 2500M was well cluttered with pipework seemingly inseparable from the demands of the exhaust-emission regulations, which intensified as the 1970s passed. *(TVR)*

The original-style 'chrome-bumper' 3000M, showing off its characteristic lines, but running in this case on non-standard Wolfrace light-alloy road wheels. *(John Bailie)*

chassis-frame was a multi-tubular design, where four longitudinal members linked front suspension to final-drive and rear suspension mountings and formed a sturdy box-section backbone. This core was linked to perimeter members encircling the passenger compartment floor, and there were suitable reinforcements around the scuttle, in the nose and at the rear. So that the old-style bodies could be used for an interim period, and because Martin Lilley could see no reason to enlarge a two-seater TVR any further at the time, the M-Series chassis' wheelbase remained at 7 ft 6 in (the figure established in 1967), though front and rear track dimensions were marginally increased.

The big difference was that the traditional 16-gauge 1.5-in diameter tubing was only retained in some places. In others, tubes of a thicker (14-gauge) wall section were chosen and in some sections of the frame there were square-section tubes; this was the

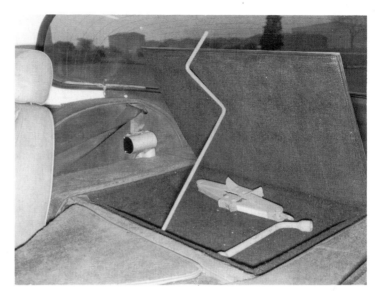

The stowage of the wheelbrace and jack in the M-Series cars was under a lifting panel in the loading area, behind the seats. This particular car was a 1976 1600M, on test. (Autocar)

Interiors changed in detail from time to time, but this was typical of the 1600M/2500M/3000M of the mid-1970s. It shows clearly the very high transmission tunnel, the shape of which was determined by the position of the frame's backbone tubes, the position of the inertia reels for the safety belts, and the reason why there could be no question of ' + 2' seating in these cars. (John Bailie)

first time that square-section tubing had been used by TVR for other than local reinforcement, and it made the structure simpler to build and somewhat easier for the bodyshells to be attached.

The front suspension was much as before, though the wishbone layout was made more sturdy by the use of the longer and more robust Triumph TR6 uprights. The steering rack was by Alford and Alder (as used on Triumph models) and the collapsible steering column was also a BL part. The independent rear suspension was similar to the superseded Vixen-type layout, but in the M-Series cars the combined coil spring/damper unit was mounted ahead of the line of the drive-shafts.

The whole frame looked more sturdy than ever before, for the four-tube backbone section was cross-braced with round and square-section tubing. It was, indeed, a frame which could easily take care of the burgeoning crash test legislation which, by this time, had spread from the USA to Europe and other territories.

A truly thoughtful feature of the new layout, made possible by

the M-Series car was the new body style. Although the new cars were still two-seaters, with no attempt even at providing 'plus-two' accommodation, and retained the same windscreen, doors and rear-window profile, they were new in most other respects and looked to the 1968-70 wide-body Tuscan V8s for their inspiration. At the front, the bonnet was longer and sleeker, partly because Martin Lilley liked it that way, and partly so as to accommodate the front-mounted spare wheel (which was a useful

A detail of the front of a 3000M, showing the Wolfrace wheels, which were only standard on the 10 special 1976 'Martin' Anniversary cars, the inner wheelarch, which kept the engine bay clean, and the rather limited opening angle of the long-nosed M-Series bonnet moulding. This is one of the later 'black-bumper' cars. *(TVR)*

the new body style, was that the spare wheel was stowed in the front of the engine bay, ahead of the engine, and above the wide, shallow water radiator. This meant that the luggage space behind the seats was now completely unencumbered by a wheel and its cover, a disadvantage which had been present in all TVRs built since 1964 with the Manx-tail style. The road wheels were in cast aluminium alloy, with 15-in rims and 5.5-in rim widths, initially to the same style as those already in use on 1971-2 non-M-Series cars. As before, the braking system was by Girling, with 10.9-in front discs and 9-in rear drums, with vacuum-servo assistance.

As far as the public was concerned, the most obvious feature of

Impressive view of the 3000M rolling chassis, polished and prepared for exhibition at the 1973 Earls Court Motor Show. By this time, the latest pattern of light-alloy road wheel, with 14-in rim diameter, had been adopted. This view emphasizes the tightly nipped-in waist of the M-Series backbone chassis-frame and shows another recognition point — the mounting of the rear suspension's coil spring/damper units *ahead* of the drive-shafts. The car in the background is a 2500M, and it is just possible to see that the Triumph TR6 type of tail-lamp clusters had been adopted by this time. *(TVR)*

Inside was a plush new interior, made instantly recognizable by the wide, high and flat prop-shaft tunnel made necessary by the layout of the tubular backbone frame. The speedometer and the rev-counter were directly ahead of the driver, while the auxiliary instruments were centrally mounted.

On the original cars, the bonnet was graced by a pair of air-intakes — one on each side of a central bonnet bulge which was smoothly blended into the nose just behind the TVR badge — and the side of the bonnet still incorporated extractor vents capped by the decorative Aeroflow grilles from the Ford Mark IV Zephyr/Zodiac models.

The new M-Series body style was the same width and height as

Overhead picture of the rolling chassis and engine installation of the 3000M of 1973, showing the very neat layout of the coil-sprung front suspension, the radiator position, the mounting of the spare wheel (which was, incidentally, something of a safety feature) and the very sturdy arrangement of square-section and round-section chassis tubes in this part of the frame. The tyre section was 185HR — 14in. *(TVR)*

The well-filled 3000M engine bay, complete with its Capri/Granada 2,994-cc British Ford V-6 engine, which could produce up to 138 bhp, should be compared with the Tuscan V6 installation shown in another illustration in this book. Among the many interesting details are the cable-operated clutch, the direct-action vacuum brake booster, the separate overflow-type tank for the cooling system and the multiplicity of pipes, hoses and wires necessary in every modern car. *(John Bailie)*

aid to providing barrier-crash resistance), with a more rectangular air-intake than hitherto to match the radiator profile. At the rear, the lines were smoothed-off very like those of the wide-body Tuscan V8s, and incorporated the Cortina Mark II tail-lamp clusters, which were now obsolete as far as Ford were concerned, for their model had been changed in the autumn of 1970.

its predecessor — for these dimensions were effectively ruled by the use of the screen, rear window and doors from the old model — but in its finalized form it was nine inches longer than before at 12 ft 10 in instead of 12 ft 1 in, most of the increase going into the front overhang, though there was a useful, if marginal, improvement in the stowage space behind the seats. One feature which was *not* improved, however, was access to that stowage space. M-Series cars, like all previous TVRs, were not equipped with an opening bootlid or rear window, a failing which began to have more impact on road testers' opinions as the 1970s progressed.

Although it was only the 2500M prototype which was displayed — and talked about — at Earls Court in 1971, TVR's plans for the use of the M-Series chassis and body style were far-reaching. An integrated range of three cars — the 1600M, the 2500M and the 3000M — was planned, and all three cars were to be launched to the British press in June 1972.

Talking about it, however, was easier than achieving it. At the time of the British launch of the three cars, only the 2500M was truly in series production, for the first 1600M (2288FM) was only then being built and the first 3000M (2410FM) was not actually started until September 1972. At the same time, too, the scene at Blackpool was confused by a handful of M-chassised 1300s, a short run of Series 4 Vixens (M-chassis, Vixen S3 body) and a considerable quantity of 2500s (now with M-Series chassis, but Vixen-style body). It was TVR's most prolific period, and one which is now remembered with some incredulity.

Once the change had been completed *in toto* — and this happy state was not achieved until the spring of 1973 — everything appeared much more logical, with three models being based on the same basic chassis and suspensions and using the same two-seater coupe body style, identical in all respects except for badging. The 1600M had taken the place of the Vixen Series 3 and Series 4, the 2500M had replaced the 2500 and the 3000M

A special high-luxury version of the 3000M, known as the 3000ML, was introduced at the end of 1973 and ran for the following year. External identification includes a black vinyl roof, sliding roof and matt black valances and side sills, while inside there was a walnut dashboard and more luxurious upholstery and trim. *(TVR)*

TVR 3000M

This magnificent cutaway drawing of the 3000M was prepared by John Bailie, a TVR owner who is also the proprietor of Image Publicity, who have close business connections with TVR Engineering Ltd. This shows the 3000M in its definitive state, as the most successful of all 1970s TVRs sold in Great Britain. Note the cylindrical fuel tank, mounted low down and at the rear of the car. *(John Bailie)*

had effectively replaced the Tuscan V6, which had died before the end of 1971.

At this point, I should record that Britain's negotiations to enter the European Economic Community (or 'Common Market', as it is more usually known) had been successfully brought to a conclusion in July 1971, and that as a consequence the British Purchase Tax system was scrapped early in 1973, soon after we actually joined the EEC, to be replaced by the Value Added Tax system already used in other Common Market countries.

The significance of this was that from March 1973 there was no longer any advantage in buying a car in kit form, as VAT was charged even when the car was sold in an unassembled state. Even though for some time Martin Lilley's policy had been to discourage the sale of TVRs in kit form (he could be more sure of the completed cars' quality and reliability), some TVR kit cars were still being sold in 1972 and 1973. The effect of the arrival of VAT was to kill-off that demand stone dead, with an upset in the demand for certain models.

The two other major factors influencing TVR's development in the early and mid-1970s were the continuing (and, indeed, worsening) series of strikes at Triumph which affected the supply of engines for the 2500M, and the disastrous fire which swept through the final assembly building on the evening of Friday, January 3, 1975.

It is now time to turn to a study of each of the three successful M-Series coupes, and I propose to take them in the order of

The 1600M, something of an orphan at TVR, introduced in 1972, dropped in 1973, re-introduced in 1975 and dropped finally in 1977. This particular car, built in 1976, is visually typical of other M-Series cars being produced at Blackpool at that time. *(TVR)*

engine size.

The 1600M

This was a model which had a rather stop-start history at TVR. It was introduced along with the other M-Series models in June 1972, but was withdrawn less than a year later. Then, following the factory fire, and in response to a change in market conditions, it was re-introduced in May 1975 and was in production for a further two years. Effectively, the 1600M was a direct replacement for the very popular Vixen series, though I must point out that the 'interim' Vixen Series 4 was on offer throughout the period when the 1600M was first in production. The only significant difference between the two types was that the 1600M was fitted with the M-Series body style and the M-Series chassis, while the Vixen Series 4 used the old-style Manx-tail bodyshell atop its M-Series chassis.

A price comparison is interesting. When the 1600M was introduced in June 1972, its basic price in Britain was £1,560, whereas that of the Vixen Series 4 was £1,425. At the same time, incidentally, the placarded price of a 3000M was £1,795 (even

though this model was not yet in production). Nine months later, when the last of the Vixens *and* the first run of 1600Ms were being built, the same basic prices were: Vixen Series 4 £1,496, 1600M £1,638 and 3000M £1,884.

The 1600M used the same rolling chassis, bodyshell and fittings as the other 1972-3 M-Series cars, the only obvious difference being that the 1,599-cc Ford 'Kent' engine, in 86-bhp (DIN) Capri GT tune, along with the excellent four-speed all-synchromesh gearbox, was fitted. So much was obvious to the casual glance, but the use of the Triumph GT6/Vitesse type of differential and final-drive casing was not. The weight of the car was 1,970 lb, unladen, which compared with 2,240 lb for the 2500M and 3000M models.

At first, to TVR's consternation, the 1600M was not a success. In 1972, a total of 57 1600Ms were ordered into production, but in the first three months of 1973 they were followed by a mere 11 cars. It was a time, of course, when there was great demand for the 2500Ms and the 3000Ms, but there must have been other reasons. What were they?

Stewart Halstead, when TVR's sales director, recalled: 'When

Even with the relatively simple four-cylinder 1,599-cc Ford Capri engine fitted (as the 1600M), the TVR M-Series engine bay is well-filled. There is one downdraught compound-choke Weber carburettor, almost hidden by the big air-cleaner, and the exhaust system is on the left side of the engine. *(Autocar)*

M-Series production of the mid-1970s, with the Bristol Avenue scene completely dominated by Triumph six-cylinder 2500M engines in the foreground and lines of Ford V-6 3000M engines behind them. That little lot represented about three weeks' supplies for the production lines, which rarely built more than 10 cars a week. *(John Bailie)*

the M-Series models were introduced in 1972 we were still making kit-cars for British customers. Then, when VAT came in, early in 1973, the home market reduced drastically. All the 2500Ms — or nearly all — were going to the States, and we

M-Series chassis-frames ready for assembly at Bristol Avenue. The frame in the foreground is likely to form the basis of a 2500M, destined for the United States market. Some sort of tyre shortage was clearly in existence when this picture was taken, for several rolling chassis are being assembled on obsolete pressed-steel rims! *(Thoroughbred & Classic Cars)*

decided that the British-market TVR should be the 3000M.'

The change from Purchase Tax to VAT had a more profound effect on specialist manufacturers like TVR than many of them have ever admitted. In 1972, TVR had sold 220 cars in Britain, but in 1973 this plunged to 101. One effect of this was that more capacity was available for export-market models (particularly the 2500M to North America), where sales increased from 168 to 287. It was a trend which Martin Lilley encouraged in 1974 for, following the 1973 Suez crisis, home sales of TVRs dropped still further to a mere 36 cars, while export sales boomed ahead to 385. It may sound paradoxical, but in 1974, the 'post-Suez' year when the world's largest manufacturers all began to suffer the effects of vast increases in fuel costs, TVR sold more cars than ever before (or, as it transpires so far, since).

The first and last 1972-3 1600Ms carried Chassis Numbers 2288FM and 2623FM, and there was then a 26-month gap in the schedules before the next example (Chassis Number 3384FM) was built in April/May 1975. In the meantime, there had been a three-month hiatus following the factory fire in January 1975. Re-introduction of the 1600M had been planned towards the end of 1974, and the press release to that effect was circulated immediately *before* the fire.

The 1600M was brought back for 1975 because TVR had sensed a big change in their *home* market as a result of the Suez crisis and the petrol rationing scares of 1973-4; customers, it was thought, might want an alternative to the lusty and hairy-chested 3000M, especially if it could look just the same. The re-introduced 1600M, therefore, had the latest road wheels — 14-in diameter, 6.0-in rim width and a revised styling pattern — along with the styling touches added to 2500M and 3000M cars in 1974. In the meantime, the price had rocketed — to £2,200 (basic) when re-introduced — and this increased progressively to £2,975 before the last car of all (Chassis Number 3938FM) was built in April 1977.

During the life of the car all the visual changes incorporated in the other M-Series cars were added, such as the deletion of the wing vents at the start of production in 1975, and the matt black sill and valance painting introduced on other cars in February 1974. In September 1976, for the 1977 model year, all the cars received a reshaped bonnet moulding, which incorporated an enlarged radiator air intake which also acted as something of a

The fire which nearly killed-off TVR and put back the development of the company by at least a year, maybe more, started after business hours one day in January 1975 and consumed several finished and partly-complete TVRs. As firemen clear up the wreckage, a disconsolate Martin Lilley (in polo-neck sweater) looks on, before taking to his bed with double pneumonia, while Stan Kilcoyne (wearing the spotted tie, in the background) looks even more depressed. Production began again inside a few weeks, but was not running full-blast for another year or so. *(John Bailie)*

Psychologically, the most important date of 1975 was the one on which the first car to be built after the fire — a 3000M — was handed over to its new owner. The twin air intakes on the bonnet top were only a temporary design feature on this model.

A raw M-Series bodyshell meets a slave chassis-frame for a fitting check before it goes into the paint shop to be sprayed, after which trimming and final assembly will follow. This was a typically busy Bristol Avenue scene in the 1970s. (TVR)

Chris Alford, genial sales director of John Britten Garages, TVR dealers in Arkley, near Barnet, giving demonstrations in his race-prepared 1600M at a Michelin International Car Test Day. Was his car wearing Michelins? I doubt it. (TVR)

There were at least as many different facia styles as there were model years at TVR in the 1970s. This was the original 3000ML of October 1973, complete with walnut panel and a very charming model. *(John Bailie)*

spoiler/stabilizer (this being more important for 3000Ms and Turbos than for the 1600M), and at the same time there was a revised facia, switch panel and tail-lamps. This was the second time that the tail-lamp style had been changed, for all M-Series models had been treated to Triumph TR6-style clusters in 1973, in place of the original Cortina Mark II clusters, but this change had occurred when the 1600M was out of production.

Exactly 50 1600Ms were started in 1975, but this figure fell to only 29 in 1976 and only a single car was built and sold in 1977. By that time, the entire market profile for TVR had changed considerably, with attention becoming concentrated on the much more powerful cars using the 2,994-cc Ford V-6 engines.

The 2500M

Although the 2500M is a little-known model as far as British TVR enthusiasts are concerned, it was the most successful car ever built by the Blackpool-based company in the 1970s. Between 1972 and 1977, a total of 946 2500M production cars were built, and the vast majority of these were sent to the United States, where TVR Cars of America (led by Gerry Sagerman) found a

ready sale for them.

The power train was that of the 'federalized' Triumph TR6, which is to say that the long-stroke 2,498-cc straight-six-cylinder engine was fitted with twin Zenith-Stromberg carburettors instead of the Lucas fuel injection found on home-market TR6s. Peak power output varied slightly from year to year, depending on the regulations and the amount of 'hang-on' gear required to satisfy the legislators, but Triumph usually quoted 106 bhp (DIN) at 4,900 rpm.

The engine was mated with the four-speed all-synchromesh Triumph gearbox (as used in the TR6 and the Stag, not to mention the 2000/2500 saloons and the Dolomite Sprint, though in the latter cases there were differences in detail), and Laycock overdrive was an optional extra and operated on top and third gears. Unlike the 1600M model, the 2500M used a Triumph TR6 differential and final-drive casing, so the chassis-frame of the TVR was modified to suit.

The first M-Series production-type chassis-frame (Chassis Number 2240TM) formed the basis of the first 2500M production car, work on which had begun in March 1972. Right

The original M-Series facia style was rather fussy and featured a padded dashboard . . . *(John Bailie)*

. . . but from the autumn of 1973 a new style was adopted, with a smarter steering wheel and yet more revisions to the heating and ventilation system. *(TVR)*

from the start, the 2500M was intended to sell primarily in North America, though Martin Lilley also marketed it in Britain until May 1973. Its original British basic price was £1,695 in June 1972, but this was raised to £1,779 in August 1972. However, as the 3000M was little more expensive and considerably faster than the 2500M, it overshadowed it completely. The consequence was that the 2500M was withdrawn from the home market and became TVR's USA-market car.

As an export car the 2500M was a great success and would undoubtedly have sold even more strongly had it not been marketed in harness with the old-style 2500 for the first year, and had not TVR sometimes found it so difficulty to ensure supplies of engines, transmissions and final-drive assemblies due to the scandalous state of labour relations which persisted throughout British Leyland in the early and mid-1970s. As it was, the total production of 2500s and 2500Ms was 1,334 in about seven years

which, on its own, must have underpinned TVR's finances through a difficult period.

Production of 2500Ms rose to its height in 1974, when no fewer than 372 works orders were issued (compared with 49 orders issued for 3000Ms); because of the fire, and a lengthy strike at BI., this figure slumped to a mere 20 cars in 1975, which dealt a severe blow to TVR Cars of America — the sort of blow which afflicted many British-orientated businesses at this time.

The 2500M was effectively under sentence of death from 1974, when it became known that the Triumph TR6 was shortly to be supplanted by the TR7 (which had an entirely different four-cylinder engine). Production of the TR6, in fact, continued until July 1976, and the six-cylinder engine design remained in production (for the Triumph 2000 and 2500) until May 1977. Supplies to TVR then dried up rapidly, and the last 2500M of all (Chassis Number 4094TM) was built in July/August 1977.

This was the padded-facia style for the 2500M and 3000M models of the 1975-6 period; a major restyle was to follow in autumn 1976. *(John Bailie)*

During its five-year life, the 2500M received many significant styling and mechanical improvements, which were always made to the 1600M and 3000M models at the same time. These show that TVR were not only able to think and act very quickly because they were a small and flexible concern, but that Martin Lilley was always looking for some way to make his cars more appealing.

Visually, the external changes comprised the use of matt black front and rear valances and side sills, with the option of a vinyl-covered roof panel, from February 1974, the addition of rubber instead of chrome facing to the bumpers from September 1974, the deletion of the front wing vents from the start-up of production after the fire in 1975 and the addition of the revised bonnet moulding for the 1977 model year cars. As far as the 2500M was concerned, however, the bonnet-top air-intakes were always retained due to the tendency of the federalized TR6 engine (like most other de-toxed units with weak carburation) to run rather hot.

The only important chassis change was that the 5½J—15-in light-alloy road wheels (of radial-spoke Vixen/Tuscan V6/2500 pattern) were abandoned in favour of 6JK—14-in wheels of a different pattern in the autumn of 1973. At the same time, the tyre size was changed from 165—15-in to low-profile 185HR—14-in.

Like other M-Series TVRs, the 2500M also received the periodic reshuffling in tail-lamp clusters and a quite confusing number of changes to the facia and instrument panel/switch/radio/heater control layouts. Early in 1974, too, better soundproofing, three additional stowage compartments, semi-reclining seats which could be folded forward to improve access to the loading area, and other details were added.

In general, of course, I should point out that many details of the fittings to US-market 2500Ms were different from those fitted to British and European 1600Ms and 3000Ms, due to the very stringent and idiosyncratic regulations which applied in North America throughout the car's life.

The 3000M
The third of the M-Series models to be revealed publically in June 1972 was the 3000M, though the first production car was

An early example of the 2500M rolling chassis, complete with Vixen-style cast-alloy road wheels and twin-Zenith-Stromberg carburettor, USA-specification Triumph TR6 engine and gearbox. Overdrive was optional and — when fitted — was located behind the main gearbox casting and immediately under the gear-lever itself. *(Autocar)*

not started until August. Without any doubt, this was the most popular British-market TVR model during the 1970s. Indeed, from July 1973, after the elimination of the 1600M, TVR announced that British and European markets would be covered by the 3000Ms, while the North American market would be covered solely by the 2500M, all of which was nice and logical — but not for long.

In the case of the 3000M, the M-Series rolling chassis and sleek two-door coupe body style was powered by the 2,994-cc Ford 'Essex' V-6 engine, as had been fitted to the Tuscan V6 of 1969-71. This engine, along with the four-speed all-synchromesh manual gearbox mated to it, was normally fitted to 3-litre Capris and Granadas, and was also in use in other specialist sports cars competing with TVR, such as the Reliant Scimitar GTE and (to a lesser extent) the Gilbern Invader. As with the 2500M and the earlier 2500 models, the final-drive was that of the Triumph TR6 (from early-1977, however, the TR6 final-drive was abandoned and its place taken by the Salisbury 4HU unit as used by the Griffith 400s and cars like the Aston Martin V8s and independent-suspension Jaguars of the 1970s).

So that costs could be minimized and service problems reduced, TVR used essentially standard engines, rated at the same peak of 138 bhp (DIN) as those fitted to Capris and Granadas. Over the years this engine proved to be remarkably durable and — in the case of the turbocharged models covered in the next chapter — receptive to drastic tuning measures.

Apart from the changes in chassis, style and trim specification given to the 1600M and 2500M models and already described, the 3000M also came in for a re-alignment in its price and specification in the autumn of 1974. At that time, fittings like the reclining seats, sun roof, tinted glass, radio and heated rear windows were all demoted from standard to optional extra equipment and the price was reduced by £235.

I should also mention two other important derivatives of the 3000M design, and one 'Special Edition'. From the autumn of 1975 (the feature was actually announced at the 1975 Earls Court Motor Show), the 3000M became available with the option of Laycock overdrive, which operated on top and third gears. It had always irritated specialist manufacturers like TVR that Ford never offered an overdrive on the Capris or Granadas using this gearbox. TVR solved it in their own way, building on the

methods evolved by Reliant for the Scimitar GTE.

Earlier than this, at the Earls Court Motor Show in October 1973, TVR showed off the 3000ML coupe, where 'L' stood for 'Luxury', and it denoted the use of an entirely changed, super-luxurious trim pack, where the facia was in wood (instead of being padded vinyl) and trim, carpets and seats were all of more expensive and exclusive specifications. However, this offering lasted for only one year and had gone by the end of 1974.

The 'Special Edition' 3000M was the 'Martin' model of summer/autumn 1976. Only 10 cars of this type were built, and they were conceived to commemorate the 10th anniversary of TVR production by TVR Engineering, the concern set up by Arthur and Martin Lilley at the end of 1965. The specification of these cars included Wolfrace road wheels, tinted glass, overdrive as standard equipment, a sunshine roof, a cassette radio and distinctive paintwork which incorporated the name 'Martin' picked out on a contrasting band of paintwork along the flanks.

Even though the 3000M gave rise to the Taimar and — less directly — the Convertible, not forgetting the exciting Turbo derivatives, it outlived both its other M-Series relatives by more than two years. The last 3000M was Chassis Number 4940FM, started in November 1979, and in more than seven years a total of 654 cars were built. The most prolific year for the 3000M was 1976, when no fewer than 161 examples were started, even beating the 2500M, whose export success was beginning to run down a little.

The life of the 3000M was prolonged successfully by a very happy series of events. In 1974 and 1975, TVR became increasingly aware that their 2500M model was beginning to live on borrowed time, as its de-toxed Triumph engine would be phased-out of production relatively soon. Stewart Halstead, who became TVR's sales director in 1975, remembers this as an immediate and pressing worry:

'In 1976 we flew out a car to Olsen Laboratories, in California. Olsen specialized in making engines "clean" for California, where the regulations were even stricter than for the rest of the United States. We were the first manufacturers — as opposed to individuals — to go to him after he had approached us and claimed to be able to "clean up" the Ford V-6 unit.' (At this time, incidentally, the British Ford 3-litre V-6 had never been de-toxed by Ford for sale in North America, and there were no plans to do so.)

'In 10 months, from start to finish, and including carrying out a 4,000-mile Assigned Deterioration Factor road test in California, Olsen made the V-6 engine "clean" for North America. We started to send the first 3-litre 3000Ms to North America in January 1977, and it carried on successfully until the last of the M-Series cars were built at the end of 1979.'

Whatever Olsen's demon tweaks were, and however they were achieved, need not concern us in detail here. However, there must only have been a marginal reduction in power and torque compared with the British/European engine specification, as *Road & Track* performance figures obtained in their December 1978 issue (actually for a Convertible) were almost identical to those obtained by *Autocar* for the Taimar hatchback in Britain.

Even by 1975, however, Martin Lilley's and Stewart Halstead's minds were on other things. They were looking ahead to modified versions of the cars which had carried TVR so successfully from 1972 to the present time. Not only were they now ready to evolve the hatchback and convertible versions of the cars which enthusiasts had been requesting for such a long time, but they

TVR's most successful works-assisted driver in Prodsports racing was Colin Blower, here seen in the lead of a group which included a Morgan Plus-8, Stewart Halstead's TVR Convertible and a couple of Lotus models. *(Roger C. Standish)*

were also ready to build a turbocharged car. All these models are so important to the evolving story that they deserve a chapter of their own.

Footnote: Important modification points for M-Series cars (1972-9)

Date	Chassis Number	Detail
Mar 1972	2240TM	First M-Series chassis built
Aug 1972	2413FM	All subsequent cars to have servo-assisted brakes
Sept 1972	2451FM	All cars to have bonnet scoops deleted All cars to have larger lower grilles
June 1973	2767FM	All 3000Ms to have 2500M road springs
Sept 1973	2851FM	New-type steering wheel fitted
Dec 1973	2951FM	1974 specification began, new seats, etc
May 1974	3096TM	Start of fitment of rubber bumpers
April 1975	3380FM	First 'post-fire' car of 1975
Nov 1975	3502FM	1976 specification began
Mar 1977	3919FM	First cars fitted with Salisbury 4HU final-drives. A few cars subsequently not with 4HU axle, but fitment became continuous from 3955FM
July 1978	4425FM	Start of upright radiator for Taimars
Nov 1978	4542FM	Start of upright radiator on 3000S Convertible
Nov 1978	4570FM	Start of upright radiator on 3000M
Nov 1979	4699FM	Last odd-number in this series
	4970FM	Last even-number in this series

M-Series cars in motor racing

Modern motor racing is a specialized business and International events can only be won by freakish machines. Martin Lilley was

If you've got it, flaunt it . . . no-one could miss the fact that this is a racing TVR, could they? Stewart Halstead, TVR's sales director, used 'Martin's Mild Mooover' — a 3000M — with considerable success on the British Prodsports scene in the late-1970s. The scene is the chicane at Croft — you can't get much closer to the circuit wall that that! (Tony Todd)

Trying really hard at Silverstone, Colin Blower gets the Team Burgess 3000M well sideways when trying to keep ahead of a Morgan. *(Colin Blower)*

far too wise to repeat the mistakes of 1962, but he was very happy to see TVRs winning in events where they could be competitive. Starting in 1975, therefore, he sponsored a small number of M-Series derivatives in the British 'Prodsports' series, where cars were not grouped by engine size, but by price. Martin had always been convinced that TVRs offered outstanding value for money, and victory in these events surely proved it.

TVR's involvement in Prodsports started with Colin Blower, who had written-off his Lotus Europa in 1974, met Martin Lilley, persuaded him to loan a 3000M for three events, and then tackled the 1975 series in a Burgess-sponsored car built by the factory. With one outright win and a number of top places that year, things were clearly promising, so for 1976 Team Burgess ran two 3000Ms, the other being driven by Rod Gretton. At the same time, TVR's sales director, Stewart Halstead, joined in with another works 3000M and between them they recorded several outright wins in BRSCC and BRDC Prodsports Championship events.

In the meantime, Chris Alford, who was sales manager of John Britten Garages, of Arkley, North London (TVR main dealers), had started to use a 1600M in the same series, which found itself in another favourable price class and also won many rounds. That car, incidentally, was eventually sold to Northcountryman Chris Meek, who campaigned it in Prodsports racing in 1979 with such success that he won the CAV-BRSCC series outright on points scoring.

With strong competition from cars as diverse as Morgan Plus-8s, Jaguar V-12 E-Types, Lotus Europas and even De Tomaso Panteras, things became really close over the next couple of years, with John Kent joining in as a works-assisted driver in his 3000M and Stewart Halstead changing to a Convertible in 1978. In 1979, everything began to come right for Colin Blower, who won many races, but finished second to Charles Morgan's Morgan Plus-8 in the CAV-BRSCC series and second in his class in the Triple-C Prodsports series.

By 1980, Stewart Halstead was really far too busy to continue motor racing seriously ('Besides,' he told me, 'Martin wanted me alive as a sales director, rather than as a dead hero!'), which was probably just as well, for Colin Blower wrote-off his Indestructible Socks-sponsored Convertible at Mallory in an early-season shunt and was very lucky to be able to take over Halstead's car for the rest of the season.

'After that,' Colin says, 'everything seemed to go our way. We won 22 races outright — every race we tackled in that car — which meant that we won the BRDC Prodsports series outright. At first we thought we'd won the CAV-BRSCC series as well, but after a lot of protesting from other people, Chris Meek was named the winner in his Panther Lima.'

The M-Series story ended there, in triumph, and (as far as TVR Engineering were concerned) at a very reasonable cost, for in 1981, as these words were being written, Colin Blower was shaking the racing 'bugs' out of a new Tasmin Convertible. In the same British series, and with the same enthusiastic support from Blackpool, it was to be a very interesting programme.

CHAPTER 6

Turbo, Taimar and Convertible

1975 to 1980

All three models surveyed in this chapter — the cars which made all the headlines for TVR in the late-1970s — evolved directly from the 3000M. In 1976-7 there was a sea-change in TVR marketing policy. Previously, one body style had been used, with a choice of engines; from mid-1977 this would be reversed, with one basic engine powering a choice of different body styles. It was one which made more visual impact on the market, even though TVR were not having to scratch around to keep themselves busy.

Chronologically, the Turbo came first, the Taimar followed and the Convertible was last of all — at least, as far as the public was concerned. Inside TVR, the idea of the Taimar was born first and there had always been the desire to build a convertible, but the decision to build the Turbo was taken abruptly, only weeks before it was revealed. Since the Turbo became a mechanical option available on *all* TVR models, I will consider it last of all and explain, first of all, how the body changes came about.

In a way, it would be true to say that TVR and Martin Lilley were bullied into developing a hatchback model — the Taimar. Not only had such a versatile body style already been developed by their rivals — the Reliant Scimitar GTE in 1968, the Volvo 1800ES in 1971 and the Ford Capri II in 1974 — but the influential magazine road testers had begun to nag about it.

It was not that TVR had never wanted to do a hatchback, but that somehow they had never got round to developing the feature. At the beginning of the 1970s the SM, or Zante, prototype confused the issue for a time and immediately afterwards there was the considerable upheaval — commercial *and* financial — brought on by the introduction of the M-Series cars. In 1973 and 1974, following the British changeover from a Purchase Tax

system to a VAT system, almost every car which TVR could make was going to the United States. However, even at the British Earls Court Motor Show of 1973, TVR were telling motoring writers that a hatchback car was under consideration and Stewart Halstead remembers that when he joined TVR in the autumn of 1975 mockups had already been built.

In the event, the launch of the hatchback TVR, dubbed a Taimar (the name, incidentally, is not *quite* that of the river which divides Devon from Cornwall), was delayed until the Earls Court Motor Show in 1976. It was, in fact, something of a last-minute launch, for the style changes for 1977 models (already described in Chapter 5) were introduced in September without mention of a hatchback derivative and the hatchback release was held back until the eve of the show itself. A study of factory records shows that the first *production* Taimar was not finished until November 1976 (after the show had closed) and was Chassis Number 3838FM. The car on show, in fact, was the second prototype, completed in 1976 — the first having been made in 1974.

Mechanically, the Taimar was exactly like the 3000M, for differences were confined to the provision of the hatchback itself. With the back closed down, the two cars were virtually indistinguishable except for the panel joint line running around the lifting panel/window and on to the lip above the tail itself. There was no external release for the hatch — a release button was very neatly and cleverly positioned above the door lock in the driver's door jamb, where it could only be operated with the door open. It followed that when the door was closed the release button could not be pressed; the operation was electric, with a solenoid operating the catch at the rear of the gate. A nice touch was that

The feature most often criticized by testers of TVRs was the poor access to the luggage space. This was finally rectified in 1976, when the hatchback Taimar was announced. With the hatch closed the lines of the M-Series car were virtually unaltered, but with the hatch open there was no missing the new feature. Ahead of the doors, there was absolutely no change to chassis or body, and behind that line the changes were kept to a minimum. *(TVR)*

The final coupe facia style of the 1970s (but not the final style of all, which was reserved for the Convertible of 1978-9) was introduced on 1977 model-year cars and included yet another relocation of minor instruments, heater controls and stowage space. This is a 1978-model Taimar facia. *(Autocar)*

this solenoid could only be 'live' when the driver's door was open, which helped to make the car more burglar-proof.

The hatch itself was bulky rather than heavy (the whole car, in fact, was about 20 lb heavier than the 3000M), hinged at the front and was supported, when open, by gas-filled struts. It did not open perhaps as far as expected, merely because it would then have been impossible for a small driver to reach the sill to tug it back down again! Once open, of course, it gave unrivalled access to the loading area, which was wide and flat, though any contents

With the hatch closed, there was virtually no evidence of the existence of this new body feature on the Taimar. In this view, the only real clue is that there are shut lines at each side of the tail, above the tail-lamps. The Taimar could be bought with the normally aspirated (3000M) type of engine, or with the turbocharged engine. *(John Bailie)*

Open wide, please! The immensely practical hatchback feature of the Taimar is clearly shown here in this studio shot. It also shows the final type of tail-lamp cluster adopted with the restyle of autumn 1976, which included yet another new arrangement of instruments and controls at the facia. When open, the hatch was held up by two gas-filled struts, and the release lock was actuated by a button hidden in one of the door jambs. *(John Bailie)*

stored there were still exposed to view through the huge rear window.

Only 15 Taimars were started in 1976, but a further 155 cars followed in 1977, which was more than the number of 3000Ms started (132) and instantly made the Taimar the most popular TVR in production. Once launched, the new TVR soon became an established part of the scene at Blackpool. Not only did it sell well in Britain, but it also did well in North America, and the last Taimars of all were built among the last batch of cars based on the M-Series chassis at the end of 1979. Altogether, 395 normally-aspirated Taimars were built in three years.

The other, equally successful, new TVR body style of the late-1970s was the Convertible. It is important to reiterate that this model was known merely as the Convertible — not the 3000M Convertible — for it had its own unique character and many special features in its construction. For all the same reasons as advanced for the late arrival of the Taimar, it took a long time

The fuel tank on all M-Series cars built from 1972 to 1979 was cylindrical in section, and was mounted across the tail of the car, low down and behind the line of the rear suspension. Access, for service or repairs, or to reveal the electrical wiring leading to the tail-lamps, was gained by removing a panel in the loading floor. *(Autocar)*

In the 1970s, many manufacturers, especially those with limited resources, had to trim their ambitions to the amount of legislation with which they could deal, in Britain, Europe and especially in the United States. In the early-1970s, proposed US legislation led manufacturers as large and experienced as Datsun, Triumph and Fiat to assume that convertible cars would soon be banned from the new-car market place — the result being that the 240Z, the TR7 and the X1/9 and Lancia Beta Montecarlo models all had fixed-head styles. In the same way, TVR, who might have been tempted to produce a convertible model, dropped that idea when they saw the smoke signals. It was not until at least the mid-1970s, when it became clear that such legislation would *not* now be enforced, that interest in convertibles was rekindled. TVR actually got their car ready for the beginning of 1978, ahead of Triumph (who similarly had second thoughts regarding the TR7, though in fairness I should quote the lengthy strike at Speke as one reason why the drop-head TR7 was not launched in 1978).

To celebrate 10 successful years of TVR production by TVR Engineering, 10 special 'Anniversary' cars, badged as 'Martins', were built in 1976. Among the obvious features were the Wolfrace wheels, tinted glass and the badging on the sides. *(TVR)*

to launch the Convertible, but there was another very important consideration — that of the rules applying to cars being sold in the United States.

The 1978-model Taimar, showing off the final development of the M-Series frontal styling, which was actually introduced for 1977 model-year cars. Without the distinguishing stripe along the side of the car, it would be almost impossible to pick a 3000M from a Taimar at this angle. *(TVR)*

However, TVR's was no ordinary convertible. *Road & Track*, in their road test of December 1978 (when, quite wrongly, they called the car a Taimar Convertible, which it most assuredly was not), dreamed up this imaginary conversation at Blackpool:

'Okay chaps. Everyone else is dropping convertibles. So let's build one.'

'Sure, but we couldn't design just another convertible.'

'I've got it, mate. We'll build a convertible and give it side curtains.'

Which sums up the design effort in only a few words. The Convertible was not merely a 3000M with the top chopped off, but a different and very genuine attempt to apply all the traditional British open-air virtues to a modern sports car.

By comparison with the conversion from 3000M to Taimar, the production of the Convertible body was a much more complex job altogether. As with the conversion of the 3000M to Taimar specification, no chassis changes were needed. Spring and damper settings were not altered, nor was the gearing, and the fuel tank remained in its usual place, behind the rear suspension, low down so as not to intrude into the space allocated for stowage. All

Convertibles, however, used a Salisbury 4HU final-drive and differential. This feature had been standardized early in 1977 for two reasons — one was that supplies of the Triumph TR6 final-drive were about to dry-up following the withdrawal of that car from production in 1976, the other being that the new final-drive was even more robust and would be able to look after the increased torque produced by turbocharged engines and by the fuel-injected German Ford V-6 2.8-litre engine which was already known to be on the way.

Much of the Convertible's bodywork, however, was different, and the easiest way to summarize this is to say that, visually at least, the changes start at the screen and work backwards. The massive lift-up bonnet moulding was the same, as was the front and centre of the floor pan, but almost everything else was different. There were special doors, a special screen, an entirely different rear-end (this was the first and, so far, the only TVR to have a separate boot compartment) and a foldaway hood. Not only that, but the winding windows of the 3000M/Taimar models had been discarded in favour of glass sliding side-screens which could be removed completely.

Arthur Lilley and his son Martin — at that time chairman and managing director of TVR Engineering Ltd, respectively — posing in front of one of the very first 3000M Turbos in 1976. It was the senior Mr Lilley's vision and — eventually — his son's application, which ensured the prosperity of TVR and its 100-strong staff throughout the 1970s and into the 1980s. *(TVR)*

There are cars which are discreet, and cars which announce their presence to the world. This is one of the latter — a fabulous 3000M Turbo, equipped with Wolfrace wheels. *(TVR)*

Hidden away under this bonnetful of machinery is the fabulous Broadspeed turbocharged Ford 3-litre V-6 engine, rated at 230 bhp (DIN) and using a maximum boost of 9 psi. The Broadspeed conversion had not been developed specially for TVR, but had first been seen on Broadspeed cars in the early-1970s. The turbocharger is tucked down, out of sight, below and ahead of the engine. *(TVR)*

The style was effectively shaped by the doors. Their tops were carved out, so as to allow arms to be stuck out into the (hopefully) warm breeze, and there was no window-winding mechanism. The glass windows fixed on with two turn buckles and when removed they had to be stowed in the boot; on early cars there was no stowage bag, an omission rectified on later examples.

The windscreen itself was no longer the familiar Consul style, but was new and special, with a bright metal surround. The hood itself was a genuine 'convertible', as opposed to a 'tourer' fitting, which means that it was permanently fixed to the sticks. Erection took less than a minute, and the car was reasonably wind-proof when all the fixings were applied.

Behind the seats there was the small, but versatile stowage area. As I have already pointed out, it was the only TVR built up to that time in which there was a separate boot compartment, and one in which the items kept there could not be inspected by other people. There was also a panel at the front of this boot, which could be removed so that more bulky or awkwardly shaped packages could be installed and allowed to stick forward into the passenger compartment behind the seats.

Apart from the obvious increase in wind noise with the hood erect, and the greater difficulty in keeping the passengers warm in inclement weather, the only noticeable drawback of the Convertible was that it was rather less aerodynamically styled than the 3000M or the Taimar, and therefore a little slower and less economical. None of which seemed to harm its attraction at all to customers, for a total of 258 cars with the normal 138-bhp Ford engine were built in rather less than two years. The last Convertible was also the last normally-aspirated M-Series car to be built (Chassis Number 4968FM) in November/December 1979.

I have not yet mentioned the most controversial feature of the Convertible, and that which brought most criticism from road-testers, which was the facia layout. Although a change was rather forced on TVR by the fact that they were lowering the base of the windscreen (the 'cowl', as the Americans call it) by a couple of inches, it was a great pity that the position of the instruments was changed so much. TVR called their new layout 'traditional instrumentation', which meant whatever you wanted it to mean. The plain fact was that the speedometer and rev-counter could no longer be fitted between the crash roll over the facia and the

Part of the pipework involved in the installation of the turbocharger. This is an experimental set-up, but the principle was carried forward to production TVR Turbos. The turbocharger itself was positioned ahead of the main mass of the engine, and the reversed exhaust manifolds fed their gases forward to it to provide power to the spinning turbine. The black-painted 'horn' is part of the pipework normally connected to the pressurized plenum chamber above the V-6 engine's Weber carburettor. *(TVR)*

steering column switch gear; accordingly, they were moved to new positions nearer the centre of the panel, widely separated, where they could not easily be read by the driver. Although one might consider the rev-counter to be the most important instrument, on left-hand-drive cars this was now completely remote from the driver's vision. *Road & Track* commented that 'the tack is so far away you can't read anything below 4,000 rpm . . .' Speedometer and rev-counter positions, however,

Turbocharged TVRs were very rare — only 63 were built between 1975 and 1979 — mainly because they were much more expensive than normally aspirated versions. Here is one of them, in rolling-chassis form, during assembly at Blackpool. The cylindrical black object near the chassis cross-member is an air-cleaner for the turbocharger intake, and the turbocharger itself is below it, hidden under the light-coloured panel ahead of the cross-member which protects the spare wheel from the heat. In the background is a mixture of 3000Ms intended for different markets — the picture was taken before the Taimar or the Convertible had been introduced. (TVR)

could be reversed if the customer requested this.

It is interesting to analyze the TVR sales story of normally aspirated-engine cars in 1977, 1978 and 1979:

In 1977, works orders were for 155 Taimars, 132 3000Ms, 76 2500Ms and a single 1600M (the last of all).

In 1978, works orders were for 129 Convertibles, 125 Taimars and 42 3000Ms.

In 1979, works orders were for 129 Convertibles, 100 Taimars and 38 3000Ms.

On that evidence, there is no doubt that the Convertible was the most popular TVR of its day, or that it was the sort of open-air hairy-chested sports car which the customers were looking to buy. All this was in spite of a US price of $15,900 for the first cars and $16,900 in 1979, and a British basic price of £5,462 in 1978, which rose to £7,007 (total price £8,730) by the time the model was discontinued in 1980. Times and prices, indeed, had changed.

However, it would be true, if somewhat unfair, to point out that

Last, but by no means least, in the M-Series scheme of things, was the Convertible, or 3000S as it was occasionally known, which TVR only built in 1978 and 1979. The rolling chassis was the same as that used on other M-Series cars, as was the front of the bodyshell, but the scuttle, windscreen, doors and entire rear-end were all unique to the Convertible. The side-windows, incidentally, slid open, and could not be retracted; instead, they had to be removed altogether. *(TVR)*

The car looks much more svelte than the background! This 1979-model Convertible had been posed on a desolate spot overlooking Blackpool sands, on a rainy morning in April. However, with the side-curtains fixed in place and the folding hood erect, the two lucky occupants would have been snug enough. The Wolfrace wheels fitted to this car were optional extras. *(John Bailie)*

Something very strange is evident here. TVR 22 is a registration number usually to be found on one of the TVR demonstrator car fleet, and in most respects the Convertible looks standard enough, but the facia and instrument layout is certainly not that normally fitted to production cars nor, indeed, to the Taimars and 3000Ms of the period. However, as I have already made clear, TVR *liked* to change their facias quite often. . . . In any case, this was only an experimental car, for there is no evidence of the opening boot, either, and all Convertibles actually sold were equipped with one of those. *(TVR)*

many of TVR's achievements in the late-1970s were completely overshadowed by the launching of the fabulous Turbo model. In quantity terms, the Turbo made little impression — only 63 cars of all body types were built between 1975 and 1979, which represents less than five per cent of production in the period — but it generated so much publicity and produced such startling performance figures for the technical press that it served its purpose as a company flagship. Was it profitable? Who knows, but it was certainly a superb image-builder, and one that no-one at TVR regrets having put on the market. In its own way, the Turbo must have demonstrated that the TVR chassis was capable of handling much more power and torque than was normally asked of it, and in this way it must have generated additional sales of the normally-aspirated models.

As far as TVR themselves were concerned, the decision to make a turbocharged engine optionally available was taken during 1975, and the prototype was built in something of a rush so that it could be shown at the Earls Court Motor Show; that prototype, incidentally, was Chassis Number 3463FM, and soon after the show it was severely damaged in a road crash as development was

being concluded. The engine conversion, however, had been in development for much longer than that, and this is where the story really starts.

The early examples of Ford's 'Essex' V-6 engine, designed and built in Britain, were neither very powerful, nor noted for their rigidity and long life. That, however, was in the 1960s, and by the early-1970s they had been refined, made more durable and given revised cylinder-heads, which released significantly more power. Ralph Broad, whose Broadspeed concern had been concentrating on the super-tuning of Ford engines since the late-1960s, turned his attention to this engine and began to develop a turbocharged unit. By the beginning of 1973, Broadspeed were demonstrating a turbocharged 3-litre Ford Capri and in the summer of that year (just before the Suez war and the energy crisis threw all such conversions back into the melting pot!) they also announced a Turbo Granada. In each case they were claiming 218 bhp at 5,500 rpm, with a peak torque of 225 lb ft at 3,500 rpm.

In the end, Broadspeed never went ahead with the production of their own turbocharged cars (and after seeing TVR's own sales of such expensive and sophisticated machines one can see why).

However, refinement of the system was carried out, and Martin Lilley finally linked up with Broadspeed, so that their engine could be used in the TVR chassis.

The engine as developed for a TVR was an extensively modified version of the 2,994-cc British Ford 'Essex' V-6 which TVR had been using since 1969, and TVR proposed to link it with an unmodified Granada/Capri 3-litre four-speed gearbox. At the rear, however, it was thought wise to specify the big Salisbury 4HU final-drive/differential and a slightly higher final-drive ratio than normal (3.31:1 instead of 3.45:1), but surprisingly a limited-slip differential was not made standard. Some were built with normal differentials, though some customers ordered the limited-slip device as an extra.

The plumbing of the engine was so complex that I can do no better than quote Gordon Bruce's comments in *Motor* of July 10, 1976:

'Tracing the . . . pipery is a job for a snakes and ladders expert, but to give you a rough idea, reversed TVR exhaust manifolds link up ahead of the engine where the turbocharger is situated. The outgoing gases then pass under the sump where they received maximum and very necessary cooling.'

Another Bruce comment which tells all is:

'Atop the Broadspeed-red rocker covers is the airtight box that keeps the carburettor pressurized; on its side, the SU-based recirculating valve that bypasses some of the flow back to the turbocharger at low speeds, keeping the impeller spinning and all but overcoming the lag inherent in turbocharged systems.'

In this developed form, the peak power output was no less than 230 bhp (DIN) at 5,500 rpm (a 67 per cent increase over the standard engine), while peak torque was 273 lb ft at 3,500 rpm, which was a 57 per cent improvement. To achieve this, and apart from the use of turbocharging boost at a maximum pressure of 9 psi, the entire engine was 'blueprinted' and balanced before final assembly, while the compression ratio was reduced to 8.0:1. It was amazing, but demonstrably true, that this engine could meet any existing European exhaust-emission requirement. Probably it could also have been adjusted to meet North American standards, but TVR never attempted this. Naturally, to keep the engine oil sump temperatures in check, an oil-cooler was needed. Testers found that the turbocharger effectively did not begin to work below 2,700 rpm, when the car performed like a

John Miles, of *Autocar,* demonstrating the way in which the glass sidescreens could be fixed, or removed, from the doors of the Convertible. Unlike all other TVRs built from 1958 to date, these side windows could not be wound down into the doors, but had to be taken off and stowed in the small luggage boot, or behind the seats. *(Autocar)*

normally-aspirated M-Series TVR.

Any of the TVRs when fitted with this Turbo engine was quite remarkably fast. *Autocar,* who tried a Turbo Convertible in 1979, reminded their readers that its maximum speed (139 mph) would undoubtedly have been higher if higher overall gearing had been specified and if the more aerodynamic coupe bodyshell had been provided. They were not, however, complaining about the acceleration, and made the telling point that the Turbo Convertible could sprint to a quarter-mile from rest slightly faster than the exotic and much more costly Porsche 3-litre Turbo.

It was the sort of car which operated in superlatives, no matter how you were considering it. Unfortunately, as far as sales were concerned, the same superlatives had to be applied to the customer's insurance costs, and to the extra price he had to fork out for the privilege of being a Turbo owner. The Turbo derivatives were available on the 3000M right from the start, and on the Taimars and Convertibles when they were announced. In the spring of 1976, when TVR were ready to deliver replicas of their own prototype, the extra cost was £2,490 (basic) and by 1980, when the last of the M-Series cars had just been built, that price had risen to £3,210. It was a credit to the Turbo, however, that when *Autocar* came to test the Turbo Convertible, they compared it with cars like the Porsche 911s, 924 Turbos and Ferrari 308GTB two-seaters. Not only was it cheaper than any of these, but it also had better acceleration and a similar maximum speed.

Naturally, therefore, this was not a TVR for everybody, and the sales figures confirm this. With TVR Engineering's permission, I have listed the Chassis Numbers of every one of the 63 Turbos built between 1975 and 1979, which show that there were 20 3000M Turbos, 30 Taimar Turbos and 13 Convertible Turbos. The most built in any one year was 22 cars — five 3000Ms, 10 Taimars and seven Convertibles — in 1978.

It was, however, a trailblazer in several ways. Not only was it TVR's first turbocharged model, but it was also the first British car to have turbocharging on a regular production basis. It also returned TVR to the standing of 'Supercar' builders, a position which they had reluctantly abandoned in 1970 when the last of the wide-bodied Tuscan V8s had left the factory.

In another way, too, it signalled the fact that TVR were now technically capable of tackling complex engineering jobs, which should have given their rivals cause to think about their intentions for the 1980s. For even while the Turbo TVRs were making all the headlines in the enthusiast press, TVR engineers were working on a brand-new car. The result was the Tasmin, and it brought TVR smoothly and excitingly into the 1980s.

CHAPTER 7

The Tasmin family

The TVR for the 1980s

In many ways, this chapter is something of a supplement to the main story. From 1958 to 1979, the development of the TVR motor car followed a steady and logical course. In 1980, the arrival of the Tasmin signalled 'all change' at Blackpool, for in almost every mechanical and body detail the Tasmin differed completely from the M-Series car. At one stroke, the Tasmin changed the face of TVR, and it is certainly the project on which the company's prosperity for the 1980s has been built. No doubt we must wait for several years to see if all the decisions which were made were the right ones; all the signs are that they were.

The design, development and preparation for production of the Tasmin was the biggest and most important project ever tackled by TVR. It took three years, an investment of at least £500,000, the complete rejigging of factory facilities and a great deal of corporate resolution to put the car on the market at all. Only one version — the Tasmin fixed-head two-seater — was produced at first, but within a year it was joined by the Tasmin Convertible and the Tasmin +2. With a further expansion of production, and with an eye to opening-up new export markets, more exciting derivatives were expected in the next year or so.

By 1976, TVR Engineering had recovered from the factory fire, were back in full production and were on the way to developing a full range of models. Not only were three engines — 1600, 2500 and 3000 — available, but the Turbo derivatives had been launched, the hatchback Taimar was about to be announced and the Convertible was under development. After more than 10 years of control at TVR, Martin Lilley was ready to consider a radically new model. The name he chose — Tasmin — was not only influnced by the similarity of Maserati's Khamsin, but also by the name of a very charming girl — Tamsin — whom Martin knew at the time.

Not only did Lilley want to replace the successful M-Series models, but he wanted to fight for markets which were progressively being abandoned by Triumph and MG. It was not without significance that in 1976 the MGB GT V8 was dropped and it had become clear that the high-performance derivatives of the Triumph TR7 were in danger of cancellation.

By 1977 he had commissioned a freelance engineer-stylist, Oliver Winterbottom, to produce a new design (for the designer of the M-Series chassis, Mike Bigland, had long since left TVR), and by the end of that year Winterbottom was devoting all his time to the project. Ian Jones, also ex-Lotus, designed the chassis and running gear to TVR's requirements. Oliver, incidentally, had started his motor industry career at Jaguar as an apprentice, later joined that company's styling division, and had been styling manager at Lotus when the Elite and Eclat models were being shaped in the early-1970s. The prototype was on the road in 1978 (TVR now had a separate development factory near Preston), tooling went ahead in 1979 and the first production cars were started in November 1979. Announcement of the fixed-head model came in January 1980, with the drophead and +2 versions being unveiled just in time for showing at the British NEC Motor Show in October 1980. All three versions were in production as this book first went to press in 1981; many more followed in the next few years.

Although the fixed-head model was announced first, the design of all three was progressed at the same time. However, for all practical purposes it was only desirable to build a single model during most of 1980, as this would not only allow the 100-strong workforce to get thoroughly used to the little ways of the new

Detail touches in the new two-seater TVR Tasmin Coupe included twin exhaust tail-pipes poking out through body apertures, the use of Ford Capri tail-lamps, the special cast-alloy road wheels and the full-width glass panel in the tail, below the normal lift-up hatchback glass door. *TVR)*

The TVR for the 1980s — the Tasmin Coupe, announced in January 1980. Virtually every part of the car was different from those used in the M-Series models of the 1970s, but the design philosophy of using a multi-tubular backbone chassis-frame, a glass-fibre bodyshell, all-independent suspension and Ford power train had been retained. The car was designed for TVR by Oliver Winterbottom, an ex-Jaguar stylist and the person responsible for the shape of the Lotus Elite and Eclat models of the 1970s. The car illustrated is one of the first few Tasmins built, and is the closed two-seater derivative. Subsequently, +2 and Convertible versions, all designed at the same time, were revealed. *(TVR)*

The impressive frontal aspect of the original Tasmin Coupe, showing the retracted head-lamp pods, the louvred bonnet moulding, which was shared by the Tasmin Convertible but *not* by the +2 derivative, and the neatly styled bonnet bulge necessary to give clearance over the Ford V-6 engine. *(TVR)*

design, but would also allow the broadest spectrum of existing TVR customers to be served immediately. Although it was always understood that a three-model range would appear, it was also accepted that they could not all be announced at once.

In its design philosophy and general layout the Tasmin was the same sort of car as the M-Series which it superseded, except that the +2 derivative was entirely new to TVR. The basis of the car was a multi-tubular chassis-frame, the bodyshells were built in glass-fibre, while competitive service and maintenance costs were ensured by the use of Ford engines and transmissions. There was no direct replacement for the 3000M (which had no lifting tailgate), for customers now demanded direct access to the storage space behind the seats; the Tasmin fixed-head model, therefore, replaced the Taimar and one Convertible took over from the other.

Like the superseded M-Series models, the Tasmin's chassis-frame is the nearest possible equivalent of a spaceframe, and uses the traditional (by TVR standards) 1½-in diameter, 14-gauge steel tubes. It is entirely different in detail, however, and has a longer (7-ft 10-in) wheelbase than the M-Series frame, while retaining the four-tube backbone type of layout, allied to the use of perimeter tubes to support the floor. The longer wheelbase not only allowed the +2 configuration to be considered, but it also enabled more front seat space to be provided, particularly in terms of the seat back-to-steering wheel dimension. As usual, there was all-independent coil-spring suspension, but in the Tasmin there were current-model Ford Cortina wishbones at the front, and the rear

suspension was all-TVR, with a trailing-arm geometry quite clearly inspired by that of the Lotus Elite/Eclat with which Oliver Winterbottom and Ian Jones were previously linked.

The rack-and-pinion steering came from the Ford Cortina, while the four-wheel Girling disc brakes featured an inboard mounting at the rear, where the calipers were fixed to the Salisbury 4HU final-drive and differential carrier, itself as used on all 3000M/Taimar/Convertible models from March 1977 and shared with such patrician cars as the XJ Jaguars and Aston Martins and Lagondas. The special cast-alloy bolt-on road wheels (there was no wire-wheel option) had 7.0-in rim widths and the 205-section tyres had a squat 60 per cent aspect ratio.

Like British Ford Granadas built since the autumn of 1977, the 1980-1 Reliants and — from the spring of 1981 — certain Ford Capris, the Tasmin used the German Ford V-6 engine of 2,792 cc. However, it is important to realize not only that the German V-6 is entirely different in detail from the British 'Essex' Ford V-6 engine used on the M-Series TVRs, which had different cylinder dimensions and an entirely different cast-iron cylinder block, but that it is considerably more powerful than the old 2,994-cc unit.

The stubby and distinctive tail-end of the original two-seater TVR Tasmin, revealed in 1980 as the car to replace the M-Series models. *(TVR)*

Lots of straight lines and a walnut-veneer dashboard, with a full range of instruments and controls, in the TVR Tasmin announced in 1980. The facia was standardized for all three initial derivatives. Completely characteristic of all TVRs was the high and wide transmission tunnel, which hid the main longitudinal tubes of the backbone chassis-frame. Electric windows were standard, and their operating switches were housed in the centre console behind the gear-lever. On original cars the handbrake was positioned vertically alongside the gear-lever (in this picture it is almost completely hidden), but by 1981 it had been repositioned in a horizontal attitude. *(TVR)*

The Tasmin's engine featured Bosch K-Jetronic fuel injection (that of the Granada 2.8i and Capri 2.8 Injection models) and had 160 bhp (DIN) at 5,700 rpm, compared with the 'Essex' peak output of 138 bhp (DIN) at 5,000 rpm. The four-speed all-synchromesh gearbox, however, which was that of the equivalent-engined Capri and Granada models, was the same as that of the superseded M-Series TVR. There was no overdrive option (none needed, surely, as the mph/1,000 rpm rating was 22.2 mph), though the Ford automatic transmission became optional in October 1980, coincident with the release of the Tasmin Convertible and +2 models.

The glass-fibre bodyshell was built in two main moulds, joined together at the waist under the decorative strip along the flanks. Barrier impact loads were absorbed with the help of marine plywood diaphragms in certain sections of the shell, and there were tubular-steel reinforcing beams in the doors to help absorb side impacts. Although special front and rear bumpers were needed before the Tasmin could be exported for sale in North America the rest of the shell incorporated every feature necessary to allow the car

The facia and instrument layout of the TVR Tasmin of 1980, complete with a BL steering column and controls, pedals and various switches. Many of the minor controls, however, were Ford-sourced, which was appropriate as Ford engines and transmissions were also used. *(TVR)*

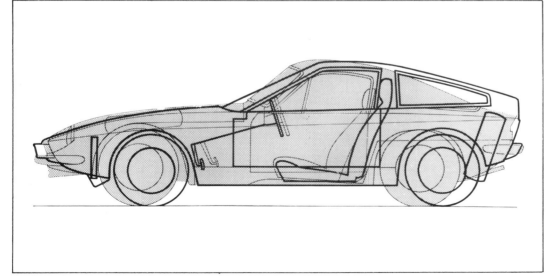

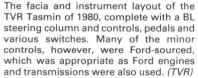

This 'ghosted' comparison shows the difference in profile between the old M-Series TVRs and the Tasmin two-seater of 1980. The Tasmin had a longer wheelbase (7 ft 10 in, instead of 7 ft 6 in), a much more steeply raked windscreen and rather more interior space. The tail was higher, which meant that there was more stowage space, and the spare wheel was in the extreme tail, rather than being in the extreme nose, as on M-Series models. *(Autocar)*

The 1980 Tasmin's independent front suspension, of which the general geometry, wishbones, uprights and brakes all came from the latest-model Ford Cortina. Spring and damper rates, of course, were entirely special. The anti-roll bar ran behind the line of the front 'axle', and is not visible in this picture. *(TVR)*

wheelbase tubular chassis-frame, there were considerable differences between the bodies, which did not even always share the same doors or nose section. To explain this, I had better start by defining the original fixed-head coupe (on which, in any case, most of the initial development was done) as the 'base' model.

The Tasmin Convertible shared the same basic front-end mouldings as the fixed-head car, but had a modified windscreen surround, different door skins (which sweep up towards the rear) and an entirely different upper tail-section incorporating a separate stowage area and bootlid.

The +2 not only had a shorter nose, but it had a unique bonnet panel, modified front wheelarches, a different front spoiler and full-length 'running board' skirts between the wheelarches. It also had a longer tail and a modified roof line, not to mention re-arranged floor and petrol tank arrangements, so that the '+2' seating could

Detail of the independent rear suspension of the Tasmin, showing the geometry, which was derived from that used by the Lotus Elite and Eclat models of the mid-1970s. Rear disc brakes are mounted inboard. The components mounted ahead of the semi-trailing suspension arm are the fuel pumps. *(TVR)*

to comply with the world's stiffest safety requirement for years ahead.

As usual, it is interesting to see how certain major decorative details had been 'borrowed' from other large-production models to help minimize the investment in a new model. The outside door handles were from the Ford Capri, as were the combined tail-lamp/ indicator/reversing-lamp clusters, while the steering column switchgear and steering column lock came from British Leyland.

The style itself, of course, was pure TVR — or, rather, Oliver Winterbottom, with approval and influence by Martin Lilley. The headlamps were hidden away (Lotus and Triumph TR7-style) above the front bumper, while the sharp wedge nose incorporated a combined skirt/air-intake, which could be detached for easy repair or replacement after an indiscretion.

Although all three derivatives were based on the same 7-ft 10-in

The rolling chassis of the Tasmin, shared with all three initial derivatives of the design. In general layout, the frame was much as used by M-Series models, but was entirely different in detail. In particular, there was a greatly changed rear suspension, and the V-6 Ford engine came from Germany, rather than from the UK. The wheels were new and styled specially for TVR; there was no wire-spoke option. *(TVR)*.

The bare chassis-frame of the 1980 Tasmin, the front-end closest to the camera lens. Though multi-tubular, like the frame of all previous TVRs, it was entirely new and much more scientific in design. *(TVR)*

Automatic transmission (a three-speed torque converter unit, by Ford) was made optional for the Tasmin from October 1980. It was the very first time that such a transmission had ever been offered on a TVR. Note the revised handbrake position. *(TVR)*

Ready for fitment to the Tasmin is this 2,792-cc German Ford V-6 engine, complete with some of its fuel-injection equipment and the plenum chamber above the inlet gallery. The cooling fan has a viscous hub and is limited to 2,500 rpm. This engine is entirely different, in every way, from the 2,994-cc British Ford V-6 used in M-Series cars, but was used in the contemporary Ford Granada and Capri 2.8i models, and in smaller and less highly tuned form in other Fords, as well as by Reliant for their Scimitar GTE. *(TVR)*

be inserted behind the normal front seats. Like the Convertible, the +2 had different front and rear bumpers from those fitted to the fixed-head car, though the windscreen and door glasses were and remained common, as did the front seats, the instrument panel and the facia layout. The rear bumpers also became common. Such a complex, but entirely logical, layout of a model range could only have been achieved at a sensible price by designing all three cars at the same time.

Although the two-seater derivatives had twin interconnected fuel tanks, each of seven gallons, mounted at each side of the chassis backbone, immediately ahead of the rear suspension, that of the +2 was a single 14-gallon container mounted above the line of the rear wheels; this move was necessary to allow the '+2' seating to be installed without lengthening the wheelbase. The fixed-head and the +2 models both had large, full-width, glass hatchbacks, hinged at the front, in the roof, and these gave easy access to the spare

Overhead shot of the engine bay of the Tasmin, well-filled by the German Ford 2,792-cc Ford V-6 engine, which develops up to 160 bhp. It features Bosch K-Jetronic mechanical fuel-injection, the 'business end' of which is tucked away towards the front left of the bay and is identified by the bunched fuel-pipes. In almost every way, this engine is identical with that normally fitted to Ford Granada 2.8i models at that time. *(TVR)*

As with the later M-Series cars, the Tasmin was equipped with a Salisbury 4HU final-drive and differential. This was basically of the same type as used by — among others — Jaguar and Aston Martin for their current models. Like these cars, too, the Tasmin had inboard-mounted disc brakes. *(TVR)*

wheel, tucked vertically in the tail, in time-honoured Grantura fashion. A feature of the Convertible model was that it could be used with the hood and its supports completely folded away, or with a hefty roll-over bar (called a 'rear header' in TVR publicity literature) erected.

For the Tasmin, a new sequence of Chassis Numbers was chosen. The last M-Series (a Convertible Turbo) was 4970FM, with no prefix. The first production Tasmin was given the Chassis Number FH5001FI — where FH stands for Fixed Head and FI for Fuel Injection. Later in the sequence, as the Appendices makes clear, a DH prefix was adopted for the Drophead, or Convertible Tasmin, while the advent of the +2 model was signalled by the addition of a number '2' as the final suffix to the Chassis Number.

Just six Tasmins (all fixed-head models) were started in 1979, so the first 1980 number was FH5007. By the end of 1980, a total of 148 Tasmins of all types had been started, and the first 1981

A feature of the Tasmin Convertible was that the stout roll-over bar could be folded back to the position shown, so as to offer true open-air motoring in ideal conditions. Unlike the obsolete M-Series Convertible, or 3000S, the Tasmin Convertible had wind-down window glasses, which are fully retracted in this pose. *(TVR)*

New models — and new management

In the next 12 months there would be big changes at Blackpool, for not only were several new models initiated or announced, the business also changed hands. As 1981 progressed, sales showed no signs of picking up again to the 1979 (pre-Tasmin) levels. For instance, 308 cars had been sold in 1979, but only 144 in 1980.

Profitability suffered badly, and for a time the prospects for TVR looked grim. Investment in the new Tasmin was not paying off, and with the car not yet 'federalized', the potentially lucrative USA market was temporarily out of reach.

At this point, an enthusiastic Tasmin owner, Peter Wheeler (who had bought a very early example, FH 5014FI, in 1980) came on to the scene and bought control from Martin Lilley at the end of 1981. But TVR was by no means a new scene to him:

The '+2' seating of the Tasmin +2 Coupe, showing that with the front seats in their fully-back position there is no leg-room at all. Finding space for these occasional rear seats meant moving the two fuel tanks (normally on the floor of the chassis, behind the seats of the two-seaters) and replacing them by a single 14-gallon (Imperial) tank mounted above the line of the rear suspension and final-drive unit. *(TVR)*

number to be started was FH5148FI2 — a +2 model. Then, in the spring of 1981, after 18 months' production, the original two-seater fixed-head bodyshell was discontinued, and in its place the Series 2 Coupe was given a two-seater derivative of the short-nose/long-tail +2 bodyshell, which meant that it had the different bonnet and front spoiler and was given the 'running board' skirts. Inside the car, however, the twin fuel-tank installation was retained and a new glass-fibre boot-floor moulding was grafted in to provide more than 16 cu ft of carrying capacity. The Convertible bodyshell, however, was not changed. The last 'Series 1' two-seater fixed-head Tasmin was FH5196FI and was started in March 1981, while the first Series 2 version was FH5211FIT, started in April. That chassis suffix (FIT, where the T stood for Series 2), was soon altered, and from June 1981 Series 2 fixed-heads have numbers like 2FH5232FI. It is worth noting that the 200th Tasmin was built in April 1981.

A great deal of ingenuity went into arranging for a +2 version of the Tasmin Coupe to be possible without ruining the lines. The car was immediately recognizable at first by the different front spoiler and by the moulded 'running boards' under the doors, but it should also be noted that the nose ahead of the front wheels was shorter than on other Tasmins, that there was an entirely different bonnet moulding without louvres, and that the detail shaping of the rear quarters was also subtly changed. Compared with the original two-seater Coupe Tasmin, the +2 version was three inches longer overall. The doors, incidentally, are the same as those of the two-seater Tasmin. This bodyshell was adopted for the two-seater Tasmin Coupe in May 1981. *(TVR)*

A detail of the +2 Coupe, showing the radio loudspeaker position, the inertia-reel safety belt pivot, and the almost complete lack of leg-room in the back. *(TVR)*

'Initially I bought a Taimar Turbo, had it serviced here in Blackpool, and gradually came to know people and be drawn into the company's activities. It was Stewart Halstead who actually got me involved, and I became a major shareholder when I saw that there were certain problems which I could help to solve.'

Peter Wheeler was a graduate chemical engineer who had started his first business in 1972 with a capital of £200. He then made his fortune supplying specialist equipment to the booming North Sea oil industry. When he took control at TVR, less than 10 years later, he was 38 years old. He became TVR's chairman, and appointed Stewart Halstead as managing director.

As Stewart told me:

'Soon after Peter took over, we established a five-year plan, and one of my first priorities was to improve the build quality and our own manufacturing content even further. The Tasmin chassis is excellent, and we wouldn't want to replace it yet, not for several years. It is a very versatile frame.'

That five-year plan, and the versatility of the chassis design, was gradually unveiled in the years which followed.

The 2-litre Tasmin

No four-cylinder-engined TVR had been on offer since 1977, when the last of the 1600Ms was delivered, but in October 1981 the Tasmin 200 came along to fill that gap. TVR's publicity material noted the discontinuation of the Triumph TR7, and suggested that the new model could take over from it!

Development of this model had been quick and easy, for the 200 was effectively a Tasmin with an engine/gearbox transplant; in place of the Ford-Cologne power train there was a 101-bhp 1,993 cc Ford 'Pinto' (officially 'T88') overhead-cam four-cylinder engine and four-speed gearbox, as normally found in the Capri 2000 and Cortina 2000 models. Compared with the 2.8-litre models, the performance was somewhat reduced, though TVR claimed a top speed of 115 mph, with 0-60 mph acceleration in 9.0 seconds.

The 2-litre engine was available for the Tasmin in two-seater Coupe or Convertible form, but was never offered with the '+2' seating arrangement, and the only significant chassis change was the fitment of reduced-section tyres on 6.0 in wheel rims. To get the

price down to an astonishingly low £9,885 for the Convertible, and £9,985 for the Coupe, a few of the original Tasmin's 'frills' were deleted — there were no electric window lifts or radio/cassette player — but the rolling chassis was the same as before.

The rationale behind the 200 was Martin Lilley's way of bringing Tasmin prices back to the level of the 1979 Taimar, and it was hoped that the sub-£10,000 price would make it an attractive 'businessman's express' as well. However, although it was well received, it did not sell as well as had been hoped, but as the 200 made very little money for TVR in any case, this may have been just as well. Peter Wheeler was actually quite irritated by the 200's sales rate, saying that it was 'an amazing bargain', but Stewart Halstead was much more attracted to the idea of selling more large-engined TVRs to export markets, particularly North America. In the end, only 61 cars (16 Coupes and 45 Convertibles) were built, the last of all being produced in September 1984.

Tasmin Turbo

The story of this intriguing project is told in more detail in Chapter 9, but at this stage it is worth recalling that it was first schemed out

This three-quarter-rear view of the 1981-model Tasmin Convertible shows the instantly recognizable body style, the differently shaped doors, the neatly folded hood and bracing roll-over bar and the separate boot compartment access. The incorporation of the 'Tasmin' name into the body side flash is a particularly neat touch. *(TVR)*

The Series 2 Tasmin two-seater Coupe used the long-tail Tasmin +2 bodyshell, but kept its own arrangement of twin fuel tanks, one on each side of the chassis backbone, behind the seats and had a long flat loading area; the carrying capacity was increased to more than 16 cubic feet. From this view, the way to identify a Series 2 two-seater from the +2 is by the location of the fuel tank filler caps; on the two-seater they are mounted well forward, near the door shut lines, whereas on the +2 they are located further back, above and behind the rear wheelarches. *(TVR)*

The 1980s management team, enjoying themselves at a race-car testing day. Peter Wheeler (with moustache) is TVR's chairman, while Stewart Halstead is managing director.

in 1980, the first prototype (a Convertible) was built in 1981, and the Coupe was shown at the British NEC Motor Show in October 1982. In 1981, Martin Lilley was quoted as stating: 'Demand exists here and abroad for an out-and-out powerhouse that sacrifices nothing in pursuit of excellent road manners and a blistering performance', and even though management control had changed by that time, the Tasmin Turbo was revealed in prototype form a year later.

Peter Wheeler, however, was not altogether convinced that this was the right sort of ultra-high-performance car he wanted TVR to be building in the mid-1980s. The result was that the Tasmin Turbo project was scrapped, and all the knowledge gained went, instead, into the:

350i — the mighty Rover V-8-engined TVR

Although TVR's biggest project, in 1983, was re-opening the USA market with the 2.8-litre-engined cars, there were good reasons for producing a new, larger-engined, super-TVR as well. There was the fact that the normally-aspirated Ford 2.8-litre engine was at the limit of its development, and that in some potentially profitable export markets the name of 'Ford' was politically unacceptable.

Peter Wheeler and Stewart Halstead therefore looked around for an alternative source of supply, and like several other independent manufacturers, before and since, they decided that the light-alloy Rover V-8 engine was ideal. Although it was physically quite large (necessitating changes to the tubular chassis frame to accept it), it was a very simple, torquey unit; in its latest Lucas-injected 'Vitesse' form it produced 190 bhp, and no less than 220 lb ft of torque at 4,000 rpm, and could be backed by the robust five-speed all-synchromesh transmission which was also found in cars as diverse as the Jaguar XJ6, the (obsolete) Triumph TR7/TR8 and the Morgan Plus 8.

The introduction of the new Rover V-8-engined car also signalled TVR's intention to drop the the 'Tasmin' name in due course, for they liked to refer to it by the simple designation '350i' (denoting 3.5-litre engine, with fuel injection). It was also the point at which several important chassis changes were made.

Ex-Formula 1 driver John Miles, when describing the new car in *Autocar* of August 27, 1983, commented:

'Let no man say that British car manufacturers cannot respond

The Ford 2-litre T88 engine fitted very neatly into the TVR 200's chassis. It was in exactly the same tune as found in the Cortina and Capri models of the period.

quickly to a demand. At the Motor Show last year, TVR were still thinking exclusively of Ford power for their cars — including a turbocharged Ford V-6 for their new flagship.

'But an enquiry from an Arab state — where the name of Ford has almost as much appeal as Tournedos Rossini to a vegetarian — produced a lightning rethink that, with hindsight, may have opened new routes of progression for the Blackpool concern.

'The point is, the TVR 350i not only goes much better than its Ford V-6, 160-bhp fuel-injected-engine sisters, but it also has (not before time) a much improved chassis whose handling and ride conform far more to the high-performance car ideal. In truth, the TVR Tasmin 350i is a completely different motor car.' (The 'Tasmin' name was not yet dead!)

Under the skin, in fact, the chassis frame was widened by 1.5 inches around the engine bay, but there were major changes to the front suspension. On the original 2.8-litre Tasmins this had been criticized as being too soft, and there had been severe steering kickback over potholes.

To rectify these problems, the new chief development engineer, John Box, modified the Ford Cortina-based layout considerably. The original design had used a lower tie bar, operating in compression to absorb longitudinal forces, and in place of this he specified a forward-facing bar operating in tension. At the same time he reduced this bar's inward-pointing angle to reduce its compliance and therefore some of the gyroscopic forces which helped generate steering kick. The anti-roll was also relocated, ahead of the line of the suspension, and doubled in diameter from 0.625 to 1.125 in, while front spring rates were increased by 17 per cent.

There was a new, large, Rover radiator up front, and although the first cars were fitted with power-sapping Land-Rover V-8-style cast exhaust manifolds, TVR soon developed fabricated tubular manifolds instead, which allowed a few more bhp to be liberated and were fitted from DH 5870RI. A few cars were built with the same automatic transmission as was being used in Rover cars of the period.

Although the original 350i was announced only as a Convertible, in August 1983, the first car had been built in March and the first coupe version in May, while the first +2 model would follow in September 1983. By the end of the calendar year, 65 Rover-engined cars had been produced, and all three body types became officially

The Series 2 Tasmin became the 280i in 1983, and in this form (note the very large shock-absorbing bumpers) it was also put on sale in North America.

The 1986-model 'federal' 280i Convertible featured these neat swept door mirrors, and had much neater bumper outlines than the original USA-market car.

The 350i model (which was briefly badged 'Tasmin' as well) was announced in 1983, and used a 190 bhp Rover Vitesse vee-8 engine. Note the front spoiler (different from that of the current 280i, and including extra driving lamps as standard).

A study in tails. The original Tasmin 350i of 1983, with a single exhaust tail pipe, was fitted with Rover-type tail-lamp clusters (left), while the 1985/1986 variety (right) had twin exhaust tail pipes, and Renault Fuego-type tail lamps.

The bulky, but lightweight, Rover vee-8 engine was a snug fit in the engine bay which had been originally designed around the smaller Ford vee-6 unit.

available from the beginning of 1984.

Even though it could not be sold in the USA, the 350i was a great new TVR development, as the sales figures soon testified; production continued to rise until, by 1986, the Rover V-8-engined cars had all but taken over completely at Blackpool. The 350i, of course, was a very fast car — magazine tests quoted a top speed of around 136mph — but it could also be surprisingly economical; because it was no heavier than the Ford V-6-engined car, it was quite easy for up to 22mpg to be recorded, even while the driver was enjoying the colossal acceleration and much improved handling.

Sales trends at TVR had been changing steadily since 1981, but from the day the 350i went 'on stream' in Blackpool, these intensified. Not only did more orders come in for V-8-engined cars, but even more Convertibles were sold. In 1983, for instance, 142 cars (of 204 in all) were Convertibles — but in 1984 there were 262 out of 335 and the proportion was to increase still further in the next two years.

Developments with the Ford V-6-engined cars

A great deal of work has been done to the design of the Tasmin family of cars in the 1980s, and although most changes have been made to all the cars, for the moment I must concentrate on those of the Ford V-6-engined models. It is interesting to note, incidentally, that in 1980, the first year of production, Tasmins were sold to personalities like Tony Jacklin, Peter Wheeler and Stuart Hall (of BBC 'Its a Knockout' fame), while late cars went to footballer Gary Birtles, Victor Gauntlett (later chairman of Aston Martin) and *Fast Lane* magazine. The first Tasmin (Chassis No FH5001FI) was later registered BTJ 286X, and the first Tasmin press car to carry the company's personal number of TVR 100 (Chassis No FH5005FI) was later re-registered ECW 440W; both were eventually sold off — are they still out there somewhere?

The original cars used TVR wheels, then Momo cast-alloy road wheels were adopted, but during 1982 some cars were fitted with the 'spiders' web' pattern of cast-alloy wheel from BHS, which was soon standardized. It was around this period that the Tasmin 200 was equipped with twin fuel tanks. From October 1982, when Ford released all-synchromesh five-speed gearboxes for their cars, these were made optional (but never standard) on the Tasmin range.

The most important development of 1983 was that TVR regained a foothold in the USA market with the de-toxed 2.8-litre Tasmin in either Convertible or (much more rarely) Coupe form. The arduous certification work was shared between TVR themselves and (for engine work and other details) TUV in West Germany. Even though a three-way catalyst was required for the exhaust emissions to meet regulations, peak power was still 145 bhp (as against the European car's 160 bhp, which was in any case de-rated to 150 bhp at about this time). A four-speed gearbox was still standard, and the US cars weighed about 300 lb more than the European types.

At first, the USA market was serviced by the Canadian importer, who had been loyal to TVR for 15 years, and whose brochures wisely advised the enthusiast to 'Experience the rarity of TVR', for it was some time before supplies grew significantly. Before the end of the year, however, it was decided to service the United States directly, and Stewart Halstead eventually set up TVR of America Inc, headed by David Beesley, who had been president of Volvo-USA for the previous two decades. The operation was originally based at Jacksonville, Florida, but it later moved to Connecticut and at one time was handling as much as 60 per cent of total TVR production.

It was the success of the export drive, not only to the USA, but to territories like Singapore and the Middle East, which then led TVR to consider rationalizing the product line. During 1984, as already stated, the slow-selling 2-litre model was phased out, and at the same time the decision was taken to drop the +2 Coupe.

As Stewart Halstead admitted: 'We introduced the +2 after listening to dealers and customers. But with the existing chassis and wheelbase we really couldn't provide much space for back seats, and I think customers really expected too much.'

The fact was that with the front seats in their rearmost position on the slides, there was no '+2' legroom at all, so all that was left was a pair of expensively trimmed luggage-carrying areas. Incidentally, Murphy's Law applied to the decision to drop the +2 models; when it was announced in 1984, three customers hurried to order cars — a 350i and two 280i models! The last +2 was built in September 1985.

During the autumn of 1984, it was decided to phase out the name 'Tasmin' completely in Europe (although most TVR enthusiasts continue to quote it as the family name for the 1980s TVRs). The decision was influenced partly because there were several different engine sizes to be advertised (and more were planned), and partly because in a subtle way the Wheeler-Halstead team wanted to distance itself from the previous management and its products. Accordingly, and without fuss, the Tasmin 2.8-litre became the 280i, with no more than a few badging and brochure changes to note the junction. The name was retained on USA-market cars until October 1985.

390SE Convertible — TVR's mid-1980s Supercar

In October 1984, TVR showed that their performance ambitions had no limits. The 350i might, indeed, be a very fast car, but Peter and Stewart thought they could do even better. On a strictly limited-production basis, and originally with the help of Rover engine specialist Andy Rouse, they decided to produce the ferociously fast and powerful 390SE Convertible — and even that wasn't the ultimate stretch of this amazing sports car design.

As TVR's own press release of October 15, 1984 stated: 'A new generation of high-performance motoring is announced today in the UK . . . Top speed of over 150 mph with blistering acceleration throughout the range must surely make it one of the quickest production convertible sportscars available in the UK. . . . TVR's chairman, Peter Wheeler, intends to return the sports car to those days of high-performance motoring that fuel crises and ever increasing legislation have almost wiped out. . . .' In other words, it was meant to be an indulgence for well-off sports car enthusiasts — but it was firmly intended to be a profitable project for TVR as

By 1986, the 280i/350i/390SE cars were being fitted with VDO instruments, though the general layout was much as it had been throughout the Tasmin-family's life.

Compared with other cars of this family, the 1984/85 390SE Convertible had a deeper and more functional front spoiler, and there was a different bonnet panel, including a unique air intake on the left side.

well. In every way it was going to be a better and faster car than the still-born Tasmin Turbo.

Visually, the new 390SE was much like every other current TVR Convertible except that it had a much deeper front spoiler (which incorporated brake-cooling ducts), along with an under-tail aerofoil section, both of which were used to trim the aerodynamics. The '390SE' badging on the tail, front spoiler and flanks told 'the other fellow' about the car which had just passed him with such verve.

The secret of the 390SE, and the reason for its title, was that the Rover V-8 engine had been enlarged to 3,905 cc (by a cylinder bore increase) and totally rebuilt and redeveloped by Andy Rouse's race-preparation business. In a process which encompassed a special crankshaft, Cosworth pistons, gas-flowed cylinder heads, high-lift camshaft profiles, larger valves and stronger valve gear, Rouse produced an engine with no less than 275 bhp at 5,500 rpm.

This was backed by a stronger clutch, a Torsen gear-type limited-slip differential, 15-in wheels and 225-section VR-rated Yokohama tyres, while there were four-pot brake calipers on ventilated front disc brakes. All in all, it was an astonishing 'personalization' of an already outstanding design, but once again I leave it to John Miles of *Autocar* to sum things up so well:

'The nice memories are of the way it would lope along at unmentionable speeds on a whisker of throttle, its animal get-up-and-go, the grip and wonderfully predictable medium speed handling. You could say that happiness is £19,700, a deserted roundabout, and a 390SE to play with. . . .'

That sum, by the way, was made up of the full price of £15,540 for a 350i Convertible and £4,160 for the work done to convert it into a 390SE Convertible; the point is that the 390SE was a conversion, not a completely built model in its own right.

Because of its high price, the considerable hand-work which went into the rebuilding of the engine, back axle, brakes and bodywork, and its very specialized nature, only a limited number of 390SEs could be made. In fact, only five cars were built in 1984 and a further 13 followed in 1985. In the summer of 1986, by which time a further 15 cars had been produced, the modification of the engines had been taken over by TVR itself, and even at a UK total price of £20,937 there was no slackening of demand.

Some people, of course, are never satisfied, and have the money available to make a car like the 390SE even more special. This explains why a number of 390SEs were produced with the long-

The 1986-style rear suspension, first developed on the factory-sponsored race cars, featured a sturdy lower wishbone and radius arms.

stroke 4,228-cc Rover V-8 engine which was being prepared for forthcoming 420SEAC model, and peak power was further increased to 300 bhp; the first of these cars was built in March 1985. In 1987, however, it looked as if the 390SE was going to be overshadowed by the 420SEAC, which was not only faster, but had restyled coachwork.

1985 and 1986 — the Series 2 models

Once the 390SE had been launched, there was time to consider changes and improvements to the other cars in the range. From the autumn of 1984 (and still retaining the 'Tasmin' name for another season), the USA-specification 280i became 'Series 1½', which was an unofficial title used only inside the TVR factory. There were no important mechanical changes, but visual alterations included the use of different bumpers, a modified front air dam and Rover SD1-style tail-lamps. All of these cars had full air-conditioning (which does *not* mean that the roof could be retracted!), metallic paintwork and hide seats.

In the spring of 1985, the 350i Convertible progressed to Series 2

specification (the first such car was Chassis No DH5980RI, but series production began in April 1985 with the new VIN number identification), at which point there was subtle reshaping of the front end of the car to make it more rounded, while new bumpers, air dam and sill extensions, as already found on the 'Series 1½' USA-specification 280i, were all standardized. These changes, along with yet another upgrading of the instruments and cockpit fittings (this was almost an annual occurrence at TVR!) and standardization of central door locking and an electric bootlid release, made a great car even nicer.

Then, in the summer of 1985, the USA-specification 280i Convertible also officially became 'Series 2', with the same series of visual changes as for the 350i, and from early 1986 the UK-market

By the time vee-8 engined Tasmin-family cars went on sale, the chassis's front suspension had been modified to include this forward-facing tie bar operating in tension below the forward-positioned anti-roll bar.

car followed suit, all of which helped to reduce the number of different bodyshells which TVR had to produce. These external changes, incidentally, were made only to the Convertibles, for very few Coupes were being built by this time, and existing body styles were retained for these orders.

By the end of 1985, all cars, whether Rover-engined or not, were being fitted with Rover radiators (the Ford-engined car had previously used a different radiator), but soon after this there was an important change to the TVR chassis, when a new type of rear suspension was specified.

Developed on the latest racing car (see Chapter 8), this featured the use of a fully triangulated lower wishbone, with two pick-up points to a new upright, instead of the simpler, forward-mounted trailing-arm and lower-link arrangement of the earlier models. This not only eliminated any small amounts of torque steer which could previously be induced, but allowed fine adjustment of the suspension geometry.

The first customer car to have the rear suspension was DH169RI, built in November 1985, the next was DH222RI, built in January 1986, and after a batch had been sent to West Germany in April 1986 it was standardized on all cars.

In the meantime, all manner of important, though mainly 'invisible', improvements were being made to the cars. New features of the USA-specification 280i Convertible, for instance, included the use of Silentbloc bush mountings between chassis-frame and bodyshell, a fully adjustable steering column (height, reach and tilt), an air-blending heating-and-ventilation system, and the use of a small-diameter Spacesaver tyre. It would be quite impossible to detail the number of improvements made to the trim, instruments, fittings and decoration in recent years — but all recent TVR customers would certainly notice the changes. The bonnet panel, for instance, has been changed several times, on several models, to improve not only the looks, but the engine bay ventilation through-flow.

And yet, in spite of all this mid-1980s activity on the shop-floor at TVR, it was all only a prelude to Peter Wheeler's and Stewart Halstead's plans for the next few years. These plans were laid bare at the NEC Motor Show in October 1986.

CHAPTER 8

Expansion into the 1990s

The old reborn, the new made even better

Perhaps the latest edition of this book was prepared at exactly the right moment, for all the signs were that the Tasmin/280i/350i family was reaching full maturity at the time that the updating and revision work was carried out in 1986. During my visits to the factory, at this time, it was clear that there was a great deal of hectic activity going on; if all went well, there might be not one, but three, new models at the forthcoming NEC Motor Show — and that one, or all, of these cars might change the future of TVR in the months and years to come.

It was a rush, but the job was done, just in time. On Press Day at the Show, Peter Wheeler and Stewart Halstead looked proud, if still a little relieved. All three models were on display, though two of them, it must be admitted, were not ready to go on sale. In addition to the existing TVR range, all of which were to be continued for another year, there was the new 420SEAC, prototypes of which had already been seen on British race tracks, and of which the first 10 cars had already been delivered; the prototype of the 420 Sports Saloon; and that most astonishing of re-births, the S Convertible. Each was at the very beginning of its career, so only a brief description is appropriate at this stage.

420 SEAC

This model evolved in direct response to a demand from TVR customers for a new 'flagship' style, with more power, better roadholding and better aerodynamics. Almost by definition, the result was likely to be a limited-production machine, and if the price was to be high, so be it. Peter Wheeler was convinced that if the car was good enough, there would be no shortage of customers. In any case, the car's specification was so advanced, and the

performance potential so startling, that the £29,500 price tag looked very reasonable indeed.

The new car had evolved as a result of a company-sponsored development programme in British Production Sports Car racing. The starting point was the 390SE model, but by the time the 420 SEAC was ready for sale there had been significant improvements to the engine, the chassis and roadholding, the styling and the body construction itself.

The car's title hid one of the principal changes, for 'SEAC' stood for Special Equipment Aramid Composite, which referred to the material used to build the bodyshells. Starting on the basis of the well-known 390SE shell, which used a glass-fibre composite material, the 420SEAC style was not only redeveloped to feature a shorter and more rounded nose, flared arches, pronounced side skirts and a separate rear spoiler panel, but much of the new panelling was constructed in Aramid materials with a significant proportion of Kevlar (which is stronger, lighter, but admittedly more costly than ordinary glass-fibre).

The race cars were the first to use the new style of independent rear suspension which has already been mentioned in Chapter 7, and that fitted to the 420SEAC was the same as on other 1986-model TVRs. In addition, wheel rim widths increased to 8.5 inches, allied to 225-section Bridgestone tyres, ventilated front disc brakes with four-pot calipers, power-assisted steering as standard, and detail changes to the front geometry, springs and damper rates were all added to the specification.

Although based on the rugged and successful Rover 3½-litre V-8 design, the 420SEAC unit was even further developed and modified that the 390SE's engine had been. For this application it had a

The 420SEAC model, officially put on sale in October 1986, had its body style developed in a factory-backed racing programme. Not only was the nose shorter, and more rounded, than that of the 390SE, but there were 'running boards' along the side, and an aerofoil section behind the cockpit.

93.5mm bore and a 77.0mm stroke, which produced a capacity of 4,228 cc, and in standard form no less than 300 bhp was developed at 5,500 rpm, with a staggering 290 lb ft of torque at 4,500 rpm. In this form, TVR claimed that the 420SEAC was capable of 165 mph, with 0-60 mph acceleration in 5.0 sec. Nor was that all, for race-tuned engines with an extra 85 bhp, produced by dry-sump lubrication, modified manifolding and reground camshaft profiles, could also be supplied.

The first 420SEAC prototype began racing at the beginning of 1986, and was soon so successful that it was banned from motor sport by the governing authorities! Quite simply, it was too fast for its opposition — but that was the sort of reputation which TVR thought they could live with. By the time of its official announcement, in October 1986, 10 cars had already been produced, and customers' plans for 1987 motor sport were already taking shape.

420 Sports Saloon

The problem with the original Tasmin +2 package was that there was really no usable occasional rear seat space, so although sales and production of the +2 models died away in the mid-1980s, Stewart Halstead and Peter Wheeler continued to believe in the potential of a more practical 2+2 model, and it was just such a car which was shown in October 1986.

The basic chassis was the same as that of the 420SEAC, but for this car an automatic self-levelling device was fitted at the rear. The engine, although the same 4,228-cc size as that of the 420SEAC, ran in a slightly 'softer' tune, with a peak power output of 265 bhp.

Most of the development work went into the evolution of a new (GRP composite) body, and although this included some basic inner panels from existing TVRs, it had a completely new exterior style and proportions. The nose was different both from the existing 350i *and* from the new 420SEAC, the door apertures were also quite different, as was the tail, and there was a distinctive and rather angular fixed-head passenger cabin. The whole car was 8 inches longer than the current 350i Convertible, and TVR claimed that the rear seats were 'comfortable for two adults'.

In October 1986, the 420 Sports Saloon was priced at £24,500, though not, at that time, ready to go on sale.

S Convertible

The most unexpected new model of all was the S Convertible which, at first glance, looked just like the old 3000S Convertible of 1978 and 1979! Some of the body lines, in fact, *were* the same, but under the skin, and in many other important details, it was a completely new concept.

The car's secret lay not in its appeal to instant nostalgia, and its throwback to 1970s TVR looks, but in its very attractive price. TVR prices had risen considerably since 1979, and when the Tasmin-based 280i Convertible was dropped from the British market, in the autumn of 1986, it was priced at £15,200. Because

the new-type S Convertible was provisionally priced at £12,995 in October 1986, this compared very well with the 1986 350i Covertible price of £17,865. Quite suddenly, a new TVR was appealing to a different, somewhat wider, market.

As with the 420 Sports Saloon, production of the S Convertible was not yet ready to begin, but there was such a startling response at the NEC Motor Show that it looked as if sales would begin early in 1987.

Although the new S was like other modern TVRs in that it had a separate tubular chassis and all-independent suspension, its chassis design was completely new, and incorporated a semi-trailing-link

The nose of the 420SEAC had an altogether softer profile than that of the 390SE and, from this angle at least, looked very pleasing indeed.

Shown as an undeveloped prototype at the 1986 NEC Motor Show was this new-generation 2+2 model, which TVR called the 420 Sports Saloon. It was claimed to have a lot more useful '+2' accomodation than the obsolete Tasmin +2 coupe.

Rear view of the 420SEAC model, showing the free-standing aerofoil section mounted on the boot lid and the new shape of rear bumper/spoiler.

111

A famous style was effectively reborn in 1986, when the S Sports car was revealed. Although this had many features of the well-loved 3000S Convertible of 1978-79, there was a completely new chassis design, the 280i running gear, a new windscreen, and many other details. The *real* attraction of this car, at the time, was its very attractive price tag – only £12,995.

rear end. The fuel-injected V-6 engine and five-speed gearbox were those of the existing 280i models, though instead of the four-disc brake system there was a disc front/drum rear installation. With 150 bhp on tap, TVR claimed a top speed of 135 mph.

The body style, though superficially familiar, was really very different from that of the old-style 3000S. The *basic* lines and some of the proportions had been retained, though the air scoop in the bonnet top was new, as were the positions of the side/indicator lamps, the wheelarch profiles, the windscreen frame and many

other details. The whole car was several inches wider than the 1978-79 version, and in the reborn model there were to be wind-up door windows. Not only that, but the 1980s-style Tasmin Convertible type of fold-down roll-bar was also to be incorporated.

The next few years promised to be extremely exciting for the little Blackpool concern, and the sales figures proved, without question, that the dodgy days of 1981 and 1982 were long gone. The problem now was not how to sell the cars that could be built, but how to build the cars that could be sold!

CHAPTER 9

TVRs that might have been

More prototypes and derivatives

Every car manufacturer, large or small, has built prototypes which never saw the light of day, and most have initiated projects which never went much beyond the hopeful showing of a single car on motor show stands. TVR is no exception; there have been one-off cars, large and small, closed and open, which have been shown to enthusiasts, but were never put on sale. Each of them, in one way or another, had an influence on the TVRs which actually were built.

In the beginning, of course, *every* TVR was a prototype and it was not until the end of the 1950s that anything approaching series production was achieved at Blackpool. Then, for a couple of years, the struggle to achieve profitability was so intense (and, in the end, unsuccessful) that there was little time to play about with new models. Before the free-spending era of the Aitchison-Hopton management began, the only real prototype to be considered by Trevor Wilkinson was a convertible version of the Grantura coupe, though one vain attempt at inserting a V-8 2,548-cc Daimler SP250 engine into the trailing-link chassis had also been made (that was a classic case of trying to get a quart into a pint pot and, like all such efforts, it failed).

Brian Hopton, chairman and managing director of TVR Cars Ltd in 1961 and 1962, had many grandiose ideas, one of which was to put John Thurner's coil-spring chassis design into production under the existing Grantura bodyshell (this eventually took place during 1962) and, shortly afterwards, to discard the stumpy Grantura style and have it replaced by a new shell styled by an Italian specialist. This, however, remained a pipe-dream for some time as there was simply no money available to finance its construction.

There was also another Hopton-inspired project, designed by the aerodynamicist Frank Costin, which looked so repulsive that every true TVR enthusiast must be relieved that it was never put into production. Frank Costin was the ex-De Havilland engineer/aerodynamicist who had been involved with Jem Marsh in the evolution of the original Marcos cars, and was also well-known for his work in connection with the Grand Prix Vanwalls and Lotus 16 models. It was Costin, however, who had also been responsible for the design of a 4½-litre Le Mans Maserati racing sports car, which was also about as ugly as they come.

At the time of its conception by Costin, who had then struck out on his own, the P5 was based around the concept of a rear-mounted engine and gearbox. The prototype, started in 1962, was powered by a three-cylinder German two-stroke DKW engine and transmission (the DKW, incidentally, was a front-engine/front-wheel-drive car), though it was thought that a TVR production car might be powered by the Rootes Imp engine/transmission, which was already something of an open secret in the motor industry and was scheduled to go into production early in 1963.

The chassis might have worked as an engineering layout, but the styling of the coupe was bulbous and nasty, for Frank Costin was not at all interested in looks, but *totally* interested in the drag coefficient of his cars. The screen was low, the door glasses were huge, the pillars were thick and the wheelarches partly faired-in. It was a monster, and deserved what it got — cancellation.

Brian Hopton's 'Italian-style' project came to nothing under his management, but it sprung back into life in 1963 after Trevor Fiore (actually a British Northcountryman originally called

Trevor Frost!) introduced himself to Bernard Williams and suggested that his own links with Fissore of Turin might be the ideal way of turning new styling ideas into reality. Money, however, was the reason why Fiore's ideas could not immediately be carried out (money was *always* a problem at TVR in the 1950s and 1960s), the result being that his ideas for a new shape of TVR pre-dated those for the Elva-BMW racing sports coupe (which looked very similar), even though it was the Elva-BMW style which was first shown to the public.

The radically new TVR style, therefore, was not actually carried out until 1964 (by which time the company operating at Blackpool was Grantura Engineering) and it was given the name Trident, a title originally coined for the nasty looking Costin-designed P5. Originally, it was to have been built up on the basis of the 7-ft 1.5-in wheelbase, coil-sprung chassis, which was standard for both the existing Grantura Mark III and the Griffith 400, which dominated the scene at TVR for the moment. However, even though work had actually started at Fissore in Turin (who had, indeed, co-operated, for a fee, in the Fiore-Williams schemes), a request from Jack Griffith in North America for the new car to be powered by an American Ford V-8 unit led to the wheelbase being lengthened to 7 ft 6 in, merely to make installation of the bulky American engine that much easier.

Two Trident prototypes — both sleek fastback coupes with light-alloy bodies (production cars, scheduled for mid-1965, though this target was completely impossible to meet, were to be in glass-fibre) — were ready for the Geneva Show in March 1965. One car was altered at Arnold Burton's insistence, after the styling had been completed, so that there was more interior headroom, and carrying this out involved raising the entire waistline of the delicately styled product; Trevor Fiore, reputedly, was not amused. That — as far as Fiore was concerned — was the bad news; the good news was that the original style, the one with which he was completely satisfied, was the TVR put on display on the Fiore-Fissore stand at the Geneva Show.

Mechanically, the first Trident was really a long-wheelbase Griffith 400, but with four-wheel disc brakes. *Autocar*, which was still fighting its way out of a very stodgy editorial period, described the Trident as having 'quarried rather than sculptured lines', which was rather a sniffy way of pointing out that the Fiore style was a sharp-edged shape, rather than one with bulbous and

The original concept sketch, by Trevor Fiore, for the TVR Trident coupe. *(John Bailie)*

flowing lines. They did, however, publish a detail illustration of the way the hidden headlamps popped up from the slopes of the bonnet for night-time use. Such a layout was normal on the Lotus Elan of the day, but on true 'Supercars', of which the Trident was a typical example, the idea was new. *Autocar* also made the point that the car displayed was mechanically incomplete. However, the second car, which had been back to Blackpool for finishing-off, had then been driven out to Geneva for use as a demonstration car.

After the Geneva Show, the display car was shipped off to the New York Show, in April, and two further prototypes were put in hand at Fissore, both with light-alloy bodies and one of them to be an open version. An attempt by Jack Griffith to have the Trident known as a Griffith was turned down, and the projected June 1965 introduction date for glass-fibre-bodied cars was soon forgotten as Grantura Engineering slid inexorably towards bankruptcy.

The events which followed the closure of Grantura Engineering in the summer of 1965 were complicated. Although the Lilleys — Arthur and Martin — reputedly thought they were taking over

The first Trident prototype, constructed by Fissore, ready for display at the Geneva Motor Show of 1965. Underneath was a longer-wheelbase coil-sprung chassis of the type TVR used from 1962 to 1972. This prototype was built in steel and light-alloy, but the intention was that production cars should have glass-fibre bodyshells. *(John Bailie)*

the rights to the Trident when they bought the bankrupt company's assets, they were astonished to find that the TVR dealer from Suffolk — Bill Last (whose stand had hosted the British-market Griffith at the Racing Car Show of January 1965) — had bought the original Fissore-produced glass-fibre body moulds for the Trident, and that in January 1966 he showed off a car at the Racing Car Show which he simply called a Trident. This had an Austin-Healey 3000 chassis, underframe and suspensions, but was quite clearly a convertible version of the original TVR Trident style. Certainly it was not as sleek, nor as distinguished, as the 1965 TVR prototype because once again the wheelbase had had to be stretched to match the Big Healey's 7 ft 8 in dimension, there were big hot air outlets behind the front wheels and the headlamps were now recessed into an altogether less delicately styled nose. The prototype, like those built for TVR, was equipped with a light-alloy bodyshell, though Last let it be known that production Tridents would have glass-fibre shells.

The sale of the body style to Last had been encouraged by Trevor Fiore, who thought the rights were still his. However

questionable this might have been, by the time the Lilleys got around to considering it, a *fait accompli* was obvious. Although TVR Engineering were in possession of several part-finished prototypes, their design had been 'acquired' by Bill Last. How, when and in what detail the impasse was resolved is not completely known, nor does it really have any place in this book, for TVR's involvement in the Trident project ceased with the bankruptcy of Grantura Engineering. It goes without saying that Bill Last's presence in the list of TVR dealers came to an abrupt end, and it must have been a source of some satisfaction to Martin Lilley that the 'TVR that Got Away' was never more than a partial success for Trident Cars, no matter what engine was used to power it. It should be re-emphasized, if any casual TVR enthusiast does not already realize it, that there was absolutely no connection between TVR Engineering and Trident Cars.

Once Martin Lilley took up management control at Blackpool, he immediately started looking round for ways to update TVR's image and widen the appeal of the marque. The first way in which he tackled this was by consulting Trevor Fiore and the Fissore coachbuilding works in Italy over a new small car. There

Due to a mix-up of rights and trademarks following the financial collapse of Grantura Engineering, in 1965, the Trident design fell into the hands of Bill Last, an erstwhile TVR dealer from East Anglia. This convertible was the first further derivative of the original Fiore-Fissore design, which he called a Trident and which featured an Austin-Healey 3000 chassis, a longer wheelbase and a different nose style. *(Thoroughbred & Classic Cars)*

The original TVR Tina of 1966, based on the floor-pan, suspensions and power train of a Hillman Imp Sport; it was styled by Trevor Fiore, built by Fissore, and utilized steel for all its panels. The original droop-snoot body style was not liked, and was revised before the project was shown again in the autumn of 1967. In addition to this convertible, there was also a fastback hardtop derivative, but neither car was ever put into production due to the high capital costs likely to be incurred in tooling. *(Autocar)*

was something of a love affair between stylists and limited-production car engineers in Britain at the time, and the delicate (if flawed) engineering of the Rootes Imp engine and transmission, which was not only compact and light in weight, but had already proved to be eminently tunable for competition purposes. Martin Lilley and Trevor Fiore decided not only to use the Imp's power pack, but based their entire design on the floorpan and suspensions from the Imp saloon car. It was a time when such things were fashionable, the Fiat 850 Coupe and Spider models being the obvious market leaders.

TVR's basic mistake regarding the small car — dubbed a Tina — was made right at the start, at the design stage. It had nothing to do with the basic engineering of the car, nor with the looks of the prototype. It was simply that the steel floor pan was mated with a steel bodyshell. Unfortunately, this was not merely to get a complete car built, with a view to converting to glass-fibre for the production cars; it was seriously thought that TVR could somehow find the money and facilities to have steel-bodied production cars built in reasonable quantities and be able to sell them at the right price. It was thought to be technically impossible to mate a glass-fibre superstructure to the pressed-steel underpan (such matings, however, have since been achieved on other cars). Clearly, the Tina, having an 875-cc Imp Sport engine, would have to undersell the Grantura Mark IVS, whose 1966 Motor Show price was £988 (basic), or £998 in kit form.

The original prototype, finished off in a great hurry for display by Fissore at the Turin Motor Show, in November 1966, was a rather plain little convertible with headlamps recessed in a drooping nose behind contoured Perspex covers. Other sources have suggested that there were family resemblances to Fiore's Trident style, which was wishful thinking as there was scant evidence of the sharp-edged style of the earlier car and the scale was completely different. As with all existing Imps, it showed off the strong positive camber of the wheels at the front and this, together with the rather anonymous frontal style, made it look more like an overgrown toy than a serious project. The author, too, can recall inspecting this original car in the company of a top Rootes engineering executive, who sadly pointed out the number of points which would need attention before it could be legally sold, even in Europe. The most obvious of these failings was the

The full-scale mock-up of the SM (or Zante) project of 1971. This was to have used the new M-Series chassis and a variety of engines, and would have been the first-ever TVR to have an opening hatch to the loading area in the rear. In some ways, its frontal style was repeated by the Tasmin of 1980. *(John Bailie)*

From the rear, TVR wanted to be sure that everyone realised that the Turbo *was* a Turbo. . . .

position of the headlamps, but there were many other details.

Once seen, the Tina disappeared from public view for another year, and it was not until TVR took a stand at Earls Court in 1967 that the British public had their first look at the project. By this time, two cars had been built — the original convertible, suitably modified in many ways to include a more bluff nose and exposed, rectangular, headlamps, and a fastback coupe version of the design; both were put on display at Earls Court.

The problem, by then, was that Arthur and Martin Lilley had both become convinced that there was no way in which TVR Engineering could take on the complete manufacture of the Tina unless its all-steel body construction was changed. In spite of desultory talks with other manufacturers — TVR even tried to talk Rootes into building the car themselves, unaware, until informed, that Rootes were already studying such a project of their own design (this was why the Rootes engineer had been so

knowledgeable when I discussed the Tina with him in 1966) — no advances were made and the Tina project was abandoned. The fastback coupe is still at the factory, while the convertible is now owned by a British enthusiast.

Apart from oddities produced on otherwise standard TVR chassis, like Tommy Entwistle's Gem and a number of self-modified specially styled cars produced by TVR dealers or customers, there is one other TVR prototype which should be mentioned, not only because of its startling shape, but also because of the time it appeared. The year was 1971 and the car was the SM — later known as the Zante.

Zante is the name of a tiny Greek island, but SM stands for Specialised Mouldings, of Huntingdon, who were already famous for their bodywork fabrication for the racing car industry. On this occasion, the styling was not by Trevor Fiore (all links with him and Fissore were broken after the pretty Tina project was cancelled) but by a BL styling engineer. The author has seen similar shapes to the SM in the Rover-Triumph styling archive of the period, and let's say no more than that. . . .

The basis of the SM was a standard TVR chassis of the period, complete with the six-cylinder Triumph 2500 engine and transmission. The body itself was in glass-fibre and was a two-seater like all previous TVRs. However, it conformed to almost every current trend, with its headlamps hidden away under flaps unless needed (like many modern Italian 'Supercars' and the original TVR Trident of 1965), a wedge front style, an upswept tail and a full-width combined lift-up tailgate and rear window like those of the Reliant Scimitar GTE or the then-new Volvo 1800ES. Brian Hatton, *Motor's* styling specialist, loved it: 'With development, this car could well rival the appearance of many exotic continentals without involving the customer/builder in an exotic outlay.'

Unhappily for TVR, who were heavily dependent on sales to Gerry Sagerman in the United States, Sagerman was not very impressed and thought it could not possibly have enough performance without a larger and more lusty engine (such as a big American V8? Such engines had always been bad news for TVR in the past). This tepid response, and the overall depression brought on by the burgeoning impact of new North American safety regulations, led Martin Lilley to drop the Zante project after a great deal of money had been spent and one complete car built. The car itself was eventually dismembered and the bodyshell brought back to Blackpool. Even as late as 1976, the author saw the dusty remains of the Zante shell tucked into a corner of the factory at Bristol Avenue. From time to time, Stewart Halstead told me, thoughts had returned to the Zante and what might be done with it, but somehow work had never restarted; in the end it was abandoned, as thoughts of the new Tasmin took its place.

The star of TVR's NEC Motor Show display in October 1982 was the Tasmin Turbo prototype, which had not only a lot more horsepower than the series-production Tasmin, but also significantly modified styling. It was actually the second such car to be produced — the first had been a Tasmin drop-head, built in 1981

For the prototype Tasmin Turbo of 1982, TVR produced this modified style, with sharper-edged nose and different details.

The 1982 TVR Turbo had its single turbocharger mounted high up on the left side of the engine — all that pipework leads round through an intercooler in the nose to the usual type of Ford vee-6 inlet manifold plenum chamber. Only two such cars were ever built.

— but was quite undeveloped when put on display in Birmingham. Clearly it had been inspired by the 1970s-style Turbo, but as Stewart Halstead commented: 'The new Turbo is a more practical car than the previous one. If we can develop a Drop-head Turbo, I'd like to think that 40 or 50 a year are possible'.

The turbocharged 2.8-litre Ford V-6 engine had been developed 'in house', and was rated at 228 bhp at 5,600 rpm, with a peak torque figure of 249 lb ft at 3,200 rpm (in other words, it was slightly less muscular than the 1970s-style 3-litre Turbo), and there was a five-speed gearbox, larger and more effective brakes and 16-inch wheels with wider-section tyres to keep things in check.

The styling featured an extended 'shovel-nose' with recessed driving lamps, and a modified tail which included an integral spoiler. Initially, production was promised to start in March 1983,

and the projected price was £16,800, which compared with £13,824 asked for the normally-aspirated model.

By 1983, however, everything had changed. Peter Wheeler had inspired the development of the Rover V-8-engined 350i, which was a more practical, easier-to-build, supercar, and it was that design which went into production instead. The two turbocharged cars were sold off — the drop-head to John Britten Sports Cars and the silver coupe to Harrogate Horseless Carriages. Where are they now, I wonder?

Even today, I have no doubt that TVR is working on several new projects, for it is clearly not a hidebound, inward-looking concern which never makes plans for its future. Someday, perhaps we will see evidence of other cars which were designed but never put into production, since not all of them can come to fruition.

CHAPTER 10

Buying an older TVR

The choice, the examination and the road test

The author's aim, in this chapter of every *Collector's Guide,* is merely to offer advice — hopefully presented in a logical manner — to anyone who might be considering the purchase of a car of the type covered. Such a car may be quite old, will almost certainly have dropped out of production, and may have suffered neglect by one or more previous owners. There is, therefore, no foolproof way of offering advice which holds good for every car and every model considered. In the case of the TVR, I can only go by the experience I have amassed with various cars, new or not so new.

My first and probably most important piece of advice to anyone considering buying an older TVR is that they should get a good idea of the cars' character when they were new. There is absolutely no point, for example, in trying out a bedraggled Grantura Mark II or Mark III and expecting it to be as quiet, well-finished, or well-behaved as, say, an MGB or a Triumph TR4. Older TVRs simply weren't as 'ordinary' as that.

I hope that you will already have gained a good basic grounding by having read this book and absorbed the many facts it contains. You will also learn a lot by obtaining and reading reprints or originals of the impartial and accurate road tests carried out by the more reliable British and North American motoring magazines. In that category I would include *Autocar, Motor* and *Autosport* from Great Britain, along with *Road & Track* and *Car and Driver* from North America. The British monthlies — *Thoroughbred & Classic Cars* and *Classic and Sportscar,* for example — will also give you a 'good read' and some background knowledge, but both tend not to give as much statistical and performance data as the more 'technical' publications.

The next point to be emphasized in connection with TVRs is that the supply of older models is very limited. Although the onset of terminal corrosion has never been a problem, it is a fact that the cars were more than usually vulnerable to crash damage. Therefore, although TVRs should not have suffered structural collapse due to rusting — the glass-fibre bodies cannot rust, though they can go brittle with old age and rough use, while the multi-tubular frames have often proved to be remarkably durable and !ong-living — many may have been scrapped after a serious accident. Leaning a TVR against a lorry, or the scenery, sometimes leads to shredding of bodywork and serious distortion of the frame and, as a result, many cars (intrinsically not worth much at the time of the accident) were scrapped there and then.

There is also the inescapable fact that it took until 1980 for the 5,000th TVR to be built and that before the Lilley family started to build TVRs in 1966 only about 1,000 cars had been built in eight years. As I have explained in Appendix D, I can give no more than 'best guess' estimates of production and exports for the first 10 years of TVR's life. I would guess, therefore, that about 60 per cent of all pre-Lilley TVRs were exported (almost all of the V-8-engined Griffiths went to North America, for instance).

However, detail figures are available for the 1970s, and these show that of the 3,290 cars built, 1,740 (53 per cent) were exported, the majority of those going to TVR Cars of America. In some years, and in the case of some models like the 2500 and 2500M derivatives, the proportion was very much higher.

All of which means, inescapably, that the balance of available TVRs leans very heavily to the more modern types — the M-Series and Tasmins. Perhaps the 'classic car' mania for collecting anything, and paying inflated prices for it, passed away with the 1970s, which means that asking prices for older (1960s-model) TVRs may have returned to more sensible levels, even though there are relatively few left intact.

It is time, now, for me to stick my neck out and nominate the 'Best Buys' and point out the less attractive propositions. Please remember, however, that what follows is a *personal* opinion; it may not be yours (which means, of course, that some TVR sellers will be delighted to know it).

I have to say, straight away, that I am no great fan of the original-type 'trailing-arm chassis' TVRs. Not only was product quality often suspect — water leaks, wind-sealing, trim and bodywork finish defective — but the chassis was of a design which was neither very rigid, nor very long-lasting in retaining its settings. The suspension settings, when the cars were new and in 'as-designed' condition, gave a very hard ride. The ground clearance was limited, which could lead to the underside and the exhaust system suffering badly on unmade roads. As the suspension began to wear, play in the trailing-arm pivots developed and the result was that the early Granturas showed a

Mounted on a slave chassis-frame, this M-Series bodyshell is about to be sent into the paint shop, followed by delivery to the main assembly lines in another building. The glass-fibre bodyshells were really very simple, and many enthusiastic restorers will be able to achieve the same standard of finish on their cars. *(Thoroughbred & Classic Cars)*

A line-up of new M-Series bodies, outside the moulding shop at Bristol Avenue, prior to being painted. *(Thoroughbred & Classic Cars)*

degree of 'self-steering' which could be alarming, if not downright dangerous. Oversteer was normal as a matter of course (the fact that the wheels rolled at the same rate as the chassis didn't help this), but once the wear set in this was intensified.

Nevertheless, the early 'trailing-arm chassis' cars have a certain charm, if only because they *were*, after all, the original TVRs. They were, too, the lightest of all the models and a fair number were equipped with the advanced, powerful and efficient single-overhead-camshaft Coventry Climax engine. The Climax-engined Granturas were quite fast — as the performance data in Appendix E makes clear — but on the other hand, those fitted with the small-capacity Ford engines were not; in fact, cars fitted with the under-one-litre Ford engines were definitely qualified as sheep in wolves' clothing, for their performance was very limited indeed. I must confess that I could never understand why the builders of specialist cars were always so ready to use the side-valve 1,172-cc Ford 100E engine at all, for its design was ancient (it dated from the 1930s), its power output was somewhat marginal at 35 bhp and its attitude to power tuning was limited — it was, I can only presume, very cheap to buy from Ford! The overhead-valve 997-cc Type 105E engine was little better, though the 1,340-cc Type 109E engine (with 54 bhp) was better.

Even if I lived in North America, I would be extremely cautious when considering the purchase of a Griffith, not because I would not trust myself to deal with the enormous performance of such a car, but because I would take to heart all the known quality and reliability problems which were an unfortunate feature of these cars. Those which survive might well have been extensively improved by their previous owners, but as this might also mean that they are considerably 'non-standard' the potential buyer is in something of a cleft stick.

I would also be somewhat chary of the attractions of a Turbo, even though it will only be a few years old and was built by the very competent management team which exists at Blackpool today. The two major problems are that the engine is a highly-tuned and somewhat costly unit, and that the concern which built them has now gone into liquidation. If the engine should give trouble, therefore, you have to face the possibility of being faced with a large repair bill (turbochargers do not come cheap, nor are specialists well-spread around the motor trade). TVR relied heavily on Broadspeed, of Southam, Warwickshire, for service expertise. That company closed down at the beginning of 1981. TVR themselves can now advise on the maintenance of the engines.

Experience with other marques and the whole historic car scene suggests that the Convertible — built only in 1978 and 1979 — will eventually become the most desirable of all 'classic' TVRs, merely *because* it was a convertible; the preservers of fine and interesting cars like to have an open-topped version if at all possible. However, I suspect that the most practical of all TVRs was the Taimar, which was distinguished by the liftback 'third door', which gave unrivalled access to the rear loading area. Along with the Convertible, the Taimar was one of only two TVR production cars in which access to the luggage stowage area was really acceptable. On all other cars it required some physical strength, and a degree of suppleness, to get at the luggage from one or other of the passenger doors.

In this connection, I have to point out that no TVR built before 1980 had a sensibly-positioned spare wheel, so you'd better start developing strong biceps to heave it out when the time comes. You'll get dirty taking the spare out of the front of the engine bay

The M-Series chassis-frame in course of construction. One of the main problems facing anyone restoring a TVR may be that the frame has been distorted in a previous accident. It may be possible to jig-up the frame to make sure it is square in every respect. *(John Bailie)*

on M-Series cars, and a hernia in heaving it out of the tail of the early Granturas; in all other cars it had to share space with the luggage behind the seats. In the Tasmin, at least it can be extracted upwards through the tailgate aperture.

My favourite TVRs, therefore, judged not only on their performance, but on their practicality, are the 3-litre V-6-engined cars, preferably the Taimars, but also the very numerous 3000M models. This is not to say that I have no healthy respect for the four-cylinder Granturas and Vixens; it is merely that I like my torque delivered in large lumps and from low rpm. If I had to choose a four-cylinder-engined car, it would probably be a Ford Cortina/Capri-engined Vixen, for these cars not only have free-revving engines which seem to last an astonishingly long time, but they also have splendid light-action gearboxes. All this, and Ford service, make them a more attractive proposition than the cars fitted with slower-revving MG engines and BMC gearboxes

Will your TVR's rolling chassis be as smart as this when you have got to this stage of the rebuild? It should be, because this was the state of a 2500M, as newly completed at the factory, in 1972 or 1973. The pattern of the cast-alloy wheels, which are the same as those used on late-model Tuscans and Vixens, confirm that date, and the engine, of course, is the USA-specification Triumph TR6 unit. *(John Bailie)*

with 'crash' first gears which — somehow — had a little less 'verve'.

So far I have barely mentioned the Triumph-engined cars. The 1300 model can virtually be dismissed as there were only 15 of these cars built and I suspect that several of them will have been re-engined at some stage in their lives to give them more performance. The 2500s and 2500Ms, of course, have been the most popular TVRs in North America, which was precisely why they were developed and marketed in that continent, but they are extremely rare in Great Britain and Europe. The 2500M, in particular, is a fine car and probably even smoother than the other M-Series models, but it is by no means as fast — the fact that its engine was rated at 106 bhp, compared with the 138 bhp of the 3000M/Taimar, proves this conclusively. Nevertheless, a quarter of all TVRs built have had the straight-six Triumph engine fitted, which makes them the most numerous of all. If I lived in North America, I would still choose one of the 1978-9 cars with the

'federalized' Ford V-6 engine — if I could find one — otherwise I would be happy to settle for the silky and refined behaviour of a well-adjusted 2500M.

It would be quite impossible for me to advise on the purchase of a particular car in print, so I will not attempt it. However, I am sure it is worth pointing out that the oldest of the series-production TVRs is now well over 20 years old and that even the youngest of the pre-M-Series models is now on its way to its 10th birthday. Even though all the cars should be reasonably corrosion-proof (the tubular frames seem to last for many years without becoming structurally defective, while the glass-fibre bodies should be impervious to any sort of deterioration except that of becoming brittle in certain circumstances), they are all going to *feel* old and tired in due course, not least in the way the bodies fit together, repel the wind and rain and stay rigid and creak-free.

Restoring a TVR to its former (and proper) glory is not for the faint-hearted, but at least there should not be the heart-breaking task of getting rid of acres of rust and there seems to be a ready supply of spare parts, large or small, and the expertise to go with them; I cover this aspect of preservation in more detail in the final chapter.

Even before buying, however, I feel that a thorough road test is essential. All TVRs — and the earlier models with the less rigid frames were worse in this respect than their successors — were vulnerable to the accident which distorted the chassis, but was not serious enough to write-off the car completely. On pre-1967 models, in any case, the frame was bonded to the bodyshell, which made separation of body from chassis, to aid repairs, quite impossible. Since it is difficult to straighten a multi-tubular frame absolutely correctly without a great deal of time spent on the job (and a jig), I suspect that there are a number of TVRs running around where the alignment is not what it should be. One object of the road test, therefore, should be to assess the car's straight-running behaviour and its cornering abilities to right and left. Do not be too proud to demand to sit behind the car as it goes along, in a friend's car, so that you can observe the behaviour for yourself.

Pre-Lilley-management TVRs were not altogether renowned for the consistent quality of their construction (many of them, after all, were built by their first owners from kits), so you should always be on the look-out for evidence of water leaks around the doors and front and rear screens, and for draughts from badly matching door/bodyshell apertures. You should not expect the output of the heating and ventilation system to be satisfactory — even on a late-model M-Series car. The Tasmins, at least, are better.

Incidentally, I mention this point in other chapters, but it is worth emphasizing that you may have great difficulty in finding an older TVR which has not been 'customized' or made non-standard in some respects. This is because the glass-fibre bodies are so easily altered by relatively unskilled mechanics, at quite a low cost (you certainly could not tackle such things on a car having a pressed-steel or a hand-built bodyshell) and it may mean that 'your' car may have slots or scoops where none should exist, or standard air-intakes or outlets modified or blanked-off altogether. The heartening point to be made is that you, like the previous owner, can also change the contours fairly easily to restore the originality.

If you are still not sure you can properly 'vet' a TVR for originality, I recommend that you cultivate a Club member who knows about these things. There is nothing quite as impressive as the special knowledge held by an active member of the appropriate one-make club. The TVR Car Club is no exception — they rank specialist 'historians' among their membership.

Quite a lot will eventually depend on your need for spare parts for the car you have decided to buy, and the situation as regards maintenance and restoration, so I devote the last chapter in this book to that important subject. However, on the subject of restoration, I am sure I do not have to emphasize that dealing with the refurbishment, alteration and substitution of glass-fibre panelling is not an activity for the novice. At certain stages of the game there may be fire risks and at others there may be a danger of inhaling the fibres themselves. While I agree that it is probably the easiest material for the ill-equipped amateur to attempt to repair without investing in expensive equipment, I do beg you to take all the proper precautions before doing so.

CHAPTER 11

Maintenance and fellowship

The Club, the spares and restoration

In previous *Collector's Guides*, dealing with cars which had been built in large quantities, but had usually dropped out of production, I have had to report that the provision of spare parts and service expertise has been abandoned by the makers of that car, and that the specialist club has had to take over. In the case of TVR the situation is much more encouraging. Not only is TVR still very much in business, but a very helpful attitude to spare parts supply and the service to back them up has been maintained. Better still, not only is there a thriving TVR Car Club, but its relations with the factory are close and cordial.

It is very much easier to find, or at least identify, the spare parts you need for an older TVR than might be the case with a more common sports car. This is not only due to the fact that it is TVR's policy to keep the spares supply capability for its older cars as long as economically possible, but because the present company's Spares Department manager, until the early 1980s, was Stan Kilcoyne, who had been an employee of the various TVR concerns since 1956 and has more than a quarter of a century of TVR experience.

In preparing this chapter, I had long talks with people like Stan Kilcoyne, as well as officials and active members of the TVR Car Club. It is indicative of the close links between the Club and TVR Engineering Ltd that Stewart Halstead is the Club's President, Stan Kilcoyne is Vice President, and Carole Newton is the main link between the Club and the factory. For many years John Bailie (who prepared the splendid 3000M cutaway drawing which appears on another page) was not only a Club committee member, but also sold his professional skills as a graphics and publicity material designer to the TVR management.

Stan Kilcoyne is the historical kingpin, without whom TVR's system of supplying 'historic' spare parts would surely collapse. Not only his own memory, but the material available to him at Blackpool, is encyclopaedic, and he reckons that one way or another something like 98 per cent of all spares requirements can be satisfied. For the TVR enthusiast who wants to do his own research, Parts Manuals are available for all the cars built since TVR Engineering Ltd was set up in 1965-6, which is to say that there is full and detailed coverage of Vixens, Tuscans and their derivatives, all the M-Series cars and, of course, the new Tasmin, which does not really come into the scope of this chapter — not, that is, for the first edition.

I am sure I do not need to point out that many proprietary components — those designed for mass-production BL, Ford and similar cars — have been used in all TVRs, the Tasmins no less than the original Granturas. This means that it may be possible for items like door handles, tail-lamp clusters, steering wheels, switch gear, suspension items, brakes and wheels, not to mention major assemblies such as engines, gearboxes and the internals of the various final-drive units, to be found from other sources if the TVR factory or a TVR dealer cannot immediately supply them. A new TVR owner can find hours of harmless amusement in prowling around his new car to see what 'hang-on' fittings he can recognize; if he cannot quite place something, he may be sure that the TVR Car Club, or TVR's Spares Department itself, already has done so!

The two most major TVR-sourced items, which are quite obviously not available from another manufacturer, are the bodyshells and the chassis-frames. The bad news here, for the owners of early models, is that there is no possibility of replacement 'trailing-link' frames being made available; worse, Stan Kilcoyne tells me that no drawings of this frame are available, nor ever seem to have been done.

On the other hand, complete chassis-frames are either held in stock, or can quickly be built-up, of the Vixen, Tuscan and M-Series models, which means that there is full coverage right back to the arrival of the first coil-spring-suspension chassis-frame of 1962. I think it is fair to say that TVR would much prefer to supply completely new frames for repair or rebuilding purposes, as a frame which has once been crashed badly and perhaps 'straightened' by less than expert hands, may never be the same again.

Although no VW suspension parts are held in stock, TVR will help identify which parts are absolutely the same as those used in the VW Beetle, for which the parts supply system is extremely comprehensive. There is no difficulty in finding suspension parts for the coil-spring chassis, of whatever type, though it is pointed out that nowadays, of course, no British manufacturer is building wire-spoke wheels for new cars, and that although new wheels *can* still be found by ordering through the various specialists, the day will inevitably come when that aspect of the car becomes a problem.

The supply situation in regard to bodyshells, or removable sections such as doors and the bonnet, is even more encouraging. Because all TVRs had glass-fibre bodies and, like other cars, seemed to suffer from 'corner' damage in shunts, a whole series of part-bodyshell sections were made available from time to time and this service has continued. Complete bodies can be supplied covering the period from the first of the Grantura Mark IIIs to the present day, and almost any section or part-section is also available, given a bit of notice. Even the Mark I and Mark II Grantura bodies, which were similar to the Mark IIIs, but had differences due to the earlier chassis-frame and suspensions underneath and some detail styling dissimilarities, can be dealt with by starting from the basis of new Mark III sections, then taking advice from the factory on the further changes needed. In the case of body styles, incidentally, be sure that the car you are considering buying is original in every respect. Due to the gradual way in which Grantura, Vixen and Tuscan styling evolved during the 1960s, it is quite likely that a car may have been up-dated, or modified, by the addition of a different bonnet moulding, later tail-lamp clusters, the substitution of an instrument layout from another model, or the use of entirely different seats from another TVR. Most people like to see complete originality in their classic cars; in the case of older and once-neglected TVRs it might be time-consuming (and expensive) to return them to that state.

Most fittings and accessories for the bodyshells can also be supplied. It was good, for instance, to see this advertisement in an early-1981 edition of the TVR Car Club's magazine *TVR Sprint*: 'For Sale: Grantura rear screens. The factory have made a new batch up. Details from Stan Kilcoyne, you must know the number by now . . .' Whenever TVR Engineering identify a spare parts demand which is economically feasible to satisfy, they will do so. You don't know that number? It is Blackpool (0253) 56151.

Almost all the major mechanical components — engines, gearboxes and the like — were taken, unmodified, from larger manufacturers. There should be no lasting difficulty, for instance, in rebuilding an MG engine used in a Grantura, or even one of the older type of four-cylinder Ford units. Nor, for that matter, should it ultimately be impossible to rebuild an American Ford V-8 engine and transmission, but the wait for essential spare parts may take much longer; there are concerns in Britain, and of course in the United States, which specialize in these big units.

The supply of trim and electrical items is also fairly straightforward. TVR make their own wiring looms and can supply new looms for almost any obsolete model, given time; some looms, particularly those used in the more recently obsolete models, are usually held in stock.

Unless money is a serious limiting factor, there should be no reason why *any* TVR, no matter how old or in what sort of disreputable condition, should not be rebuilt to a thoroughly roadworthy condition, and once this has been done it should also be easy enough to make sure it is properly maintained, as the factory would recommend. Such chores are made easier by the fact that there is a great deal of factory-sourced or factory-approved literature available to cover the subject. In preparing this book, for instance, I sifted through a whole range of Owners' Handbooks which deal with TVRs of all ages, that for the original series-production Granturas — Marks I, II, IIA and III — having been reprinted by TVR Engineering at the request of the TVR

The Ford 'Kent' engine has been built in many forms over the years, but from 1967 the 1,599-cc unit was made available in cross-flow form. In this Cortina 1600GT tune it was fitted to the Vixen range from 1967 to 1973, and to the 1600Ms built intermittently between 1972 and 1977. Over the years there were many minor development changes, but the basic form, including the downdraught compound dual-choke Weber carburettor and the tubular four-branch exhaust manifold, remained the same. This particular example was manufactured in 1970. *(Ford Motor Company)*

Car Club.

Which brings me neatly along to the subject of the TVR Car Club itself. As I have said in every previous *Collector's Guide* which I have prepared, every buyer of a specialist car, especially if it is obsolete, should join the specialist car club connected with his chosen marque. The investment in annual subscriptions can pay off many times over by the special knowledge which is relayed to all members. Earlier in this chapter I think I made it clear that in the case of TVR it would be very difficult to remain in ignorance of the club, as so many factory employees, or

directors, are also influential members of the TVR Car Club.

The Club's Secretary is:
Vic Brookes
'Calderstones'
1 Brackenhills
Upper Poppleton
York YO2 6DH
Telephone: 0904 794653.

Like most one-make clubs, the TVR Car Club seeks to provide

More TVRs have been built with the British Ford 3-litre 'Essex' V-6 engine than any other type. It was usually fitted in the form illustrated, with a single downdraught two-choke Weber carburettor and about 138 bhp, but a select few of these units were extensively reworked by Broadspeed to produce 230 bhp with the aid of turbocharging. Some details of TVR-installed engines may differ from this unit, which was as normally used in Ford Zodiacs and Granadas. *(Ford Motor Company)*

spares and service information, a forum for sales and wants — of cars and components — and leans more towards the preservation of the cars in the marque and as a social club, rather than as a competition-orientated group, though interest in motor sport is growing. The main events of the year include the Annual General Meeting, the National TVR Extravaganza, which is based on Blackpool and the TVR factory.

The Club has more than 1,300 members — the number is growing all the time — of which about 150 live in the United States and Canada. There are members in most European countries, in fact in every country where TVRs are sold.

Inflation is that horrid fact of life with which we all have to contend, but at the time of writing (mid-1986), the annual subscription fee is £12.50 and there is a £1.50 joining fee for new members. Regular contact beween the Club committee and the membership is assured by the publication of the magazine *TVR Sprint*, which is published monthly.

It is not essential, however, to rely on the TVR Car Club for the supply of spare parts and expertise. TVR have appointed a chain of 10 dealers in the United Kingdom and there are 10 concessionaires overseas. The address of long-established agents and concessionaires and the telephone numbers by which they may be contacted, are listed below.

Major United Kingdom dealers

Harrogate Horseless Carriages Ltd, 284-286 Skipton Road, Harrogate, West Yorkshire (Tel: 0423 521074)

BLE Automotive, 780 Kingsbury Road, Erdington, Birmingham B24 9PS (Tel: 021 384 8565)

The Sportscar Centre, Drakes Broughton, near Pershore, Worcs (Tel: 0905 840288)

The TVR Centre, Barnet Road, Arkley, Barnet, Herts (Tel: 01 440 6666)

Luxury and Hyperformance Ltd, 120-124 King Street, Hammersmith, London W6 0RH (Tel: 01 748 0821)

Hillside Motors, 292-300 Carshalton Road, Carshalton, Surrey SM5 2QB (Tel: 01 643 9106)

Fernhurst Motor Co, Midhurst Road, Fernhurst, Haslemere, Surrey GU27 3EE (Tel: 0428 53924)

Dobshill Garage, Hawarden, Deeside, Clwyd, North Wales (Tel: 0244 545115)

Ackrill Automotive, High Street, Littlebourne, Kent CT3 1SX (Tel: 0227 720644)

PKT Motors (Rochford) Ltd, 72-76 West Street, Rochford, Essex (Tel: 037 881 3016)

TVR Concessionaires overseas

Belgium: Panimpex PVBA, Groene Biezenlaan 49, B8470 De Panne (Tel: 058-413872)

Canada: JAG Enterprises, 112 Crockford Boulevard, Scarborough, Ontario M1R 3CS (Tel: 416-752-7226)

France: TVR France, 4 Rue de la Celle, 78150 Le Chesnay (Tel: (3) 954-7732)

Holland: b.v. Nimag, Reedijk 9, 3274 KE Hinenoord (Tel: 01862-7911)

Malaysia: Autohouse Trading PTE Ltd, 80 Marine Parade Road, 11-02 Parkway Parade, Singapore 1544 (Tel: 3451911)

South Africa: House of Sports (Pty) Ltd, 72-7th Avenue, Parktown North 2193, Johannesburg (Tel: From UK, 01027-11-788-5218)

Spain: TVR Spain SA, c/o O'Donnell No 6, Madrid 6 (Tel: From UK, 010-341-252-9793)

Sweden: KP Motors AB, St Paulsgatan 25, S-11648, Stockholm (Tel: 01-8-423027)

USA: TVR of America Inc, 450 Town Street, East Haddam, Connecticut 06423 (Tel: 1800-351-4794)

West Germany: Auto Becker, Suitbertusstrasse 150, 4000 Dusseldorf (Tel: 3380-1)

APPENDIX A

TVR milestones and the family tree to date

To summarize the complex technical and commercial events which have taken place at TVR since inception, this Appendix should form a useful 'skeleton' around which the main story and the details can be filled in:

1947   Trevor Wilkinson formed TVR Engineering and built his first 'special'.

1949   First TVR sold — to Trevor Wilkinson's cousin.

1954   Austin A40-engined TVR Sports Saloons first sold.

1957   Six prototype TVR Coupes sold.

1958   Grantura Mark I put into series production. TVR Engineering dissolved. Layton Sports Cars Ltd formed to take its place.

1961   Beginning of the Aitchison-Hopton period of ownership. Layton Sports Cars dissolved and TVR Cars Ltd founded.

1962   Announcement of Mark III coil-spring chassis and short-lived competitions programme. Trevor Wilkinson left the firm in April. Bankruptcy of TVR Cars Ltd in the autumn. Grantura Engineering Ltd (a creditor of the bankrupt company and its main supplier) took up the manufacture of TVRs.

1963   First deliveries of Griffiths to the USA.

1964   Announcement of Manx-tail derivative of Grantura — 1800S.

1965   Trident prototype revealed, but lost to other hands during the year. Collapse of Grantura Engineering in August. Purchase of all assets by Arthur and Martin Lilley in November. Formation of TVR Engineering Ltd.

1966   First 'Lilley-management' TVRs assembled — 1800S models.

1967   First new-model developments — Vixen replacing Grantura 1800S and Tuscan V8 replacing obsolete Griffith 400. Tina prototypes shown at Earls Court Motor Show, but not progressed.

1968   First showing of wide-bodied Tuscan V8 SE. Body never used on any other TVR, but was effective forerunner of M-Type style.

1969   Tuscan V6 introduced — halfway model between Vixen S2 (with 1.6-litre four-cylinder engine) and Tuscan V8 SE (with 4.7-litre V-8 engine).

1970   Assembly facilities moved from original Hoo Hill factory to the Bristol Avenue, Bispham, works — completed over the Christmas period.

1971   1300 and 2500 first sold, on basis of Vixen S3 chassis and style: replaced neither Tuscan V6 nor Vixen S3.

1972   Introduction of M-Series chassis and related body style, all-new in detail, but still with coil-spring front and rear independent suspension. Pre-M-Series chassis (1962-72) immediately phased out, with no overlap. 2500M was original M-Series chassis, soon joined by 1600M and 3000M. Some 1300, 2500 and Vixen (S4) built with M-Series chassis and old body style — this anomaly cleared up by May 1973.

1973   1600M discontinued (but re-introduced in 1975).

1975   Serious disruption due to fire at Bristol Avenue on January 3, 1975. Production restarted in March/April. TVR Turbo (with Broadspeed-modified 3.0-litre Ford engine) announced at Earls Court Motor Show. Re-introduction of 1600M model.

1976   Introduction of Taimar with hatchback.

1977   Last de-toxed 2500M built (for the USA) as engine taken out of production by Triumph. 3000M took its place.

1978   Introduction of TVR Convertible — first drop-head series-production TVR, which instantly took over majority of TVR sales.

1979   Last M-Type/Taimar/Convertible models built prior to launch of all-new TVR in 1980.

1980   Launch, in January, of Tasmin — new chassis, new body style, new engine (German Ford, 2.8-litre V-6 with fuel injection) — no carry-over of components, except in minor detail, from M-Type range. Two-seater coupe at first, joined in October (at NEC Motor Show) by two-seater convertible and 2+2 coupe. Automatic transmission option announced at NEC Motor Show.

1981   S2 two-seater coupe replaced original Tasmin coupé. 2-litre Ford-engined Tasmin 200 announced.

1982   Peter Wheeler bought control from Martin Lilley; Stewart Halstead became Managing Director. Prototype Tasmin Turbo shown, but not put into production.

1983   Re-launch of TVR in the USA market. Launch of Rover V-8-engined 350i models. 'Tasmin' name dropped in favour of '280i' name.

1984   Launch of 390SE Convertible with 275bhp engine. Last Tasmin 200s built.

1985   280i became 'Series 2' in USA markets. 350i Convertible became Series 2 in all other markets. Last +2 models built. First 390SEs built with optional 4.2-litre engine.

1986   Launch of three important new models — 420SEAC, 420 Sports Saloon and S Convertible.

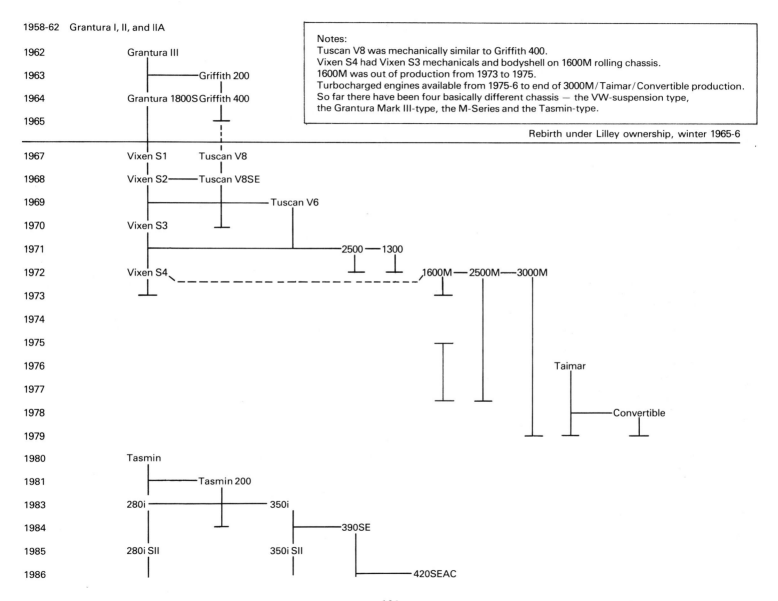

1958-62   Grantura I, II, and IIA

1962   Grantura III

1963   Griffith 200

1964   Grantura 1800S Griffith 400

1965

Notes:
Tuscan V8 was mechanically similar to Griffith 400.
Vixen S4 had Vixen S3 mechanicals and bodyshell on 1600M rolling chassis.
1600M was out of production from 1973 to 1975.
Turbocharged engines available from 1975-6 to end of 3000M/Taimar/Convertible production.
So far there have been four basically different chassis — the VW-suspension type,
the Grantura Mark III-type, the M-Series and the Tasmin-type.

Rebirth under Lilley ownership, winter 1965-6

1967   Vixen S1   Tuscan V8

1968   Vixen S2——Tuscan V8SE

1969   Tuscan V6

1970   Vixen S3

1971   2500——1300

1972   Vixen S4   1600M——2500M——3000M

1973

1974

1975

1976   Taimar

1977

1978   Convertible

1979

1980   Tasmin

1981   Tasmin 200

1983   280i   350i

1984   390SE

1985   280i SII   350i SII

1986   420SEAC

131

APPENDIX B

Technical specifications

Grantura Mark I — produced 1958 to 1960

Engine: Choice of Coventry Climax, Ford or BMC engines. Principal engine: Coventry Climax Type FWE, 4-cyl, 76.2 × 66.7mm, 1,216cc, CR 10.0:1, 2 SU carbs, single-overhead-camshaft valve gear. 83bhp (net) at 6,000rpm. Maximum torque 75lb ft at 4,800rpm.

Alternative engines: Ford (side-valve) 100E unit of 1,172cc, 35bhp at 4,600rpm, with Shorrock supercharging 56bhp at 4,600rpm; Ford (overhead-valve) 105E unit of 997cc, 39bhp (net) at 5,000rpm; BMC (MGA-type, overhead-valve) unit of 1,489cc, 72bhp (net) at 5,500rpm, or Coventry Climax (overhead-camshaft) Type FWA of 1,098cc, various power outputs.

Transmission: Axle ratio 4.70:1 with Coventry Climax engine, other ratios between 4.1:1 and 5.1:1 also available depending on engine option chosen, hypoid-bevel gears. Four-speed BMC B-Series gearbox with Coventry Climax and MGA engines, three-speed Ford gearbox with 100E side-valve engine, four-speed Ford gearbox with 105E overhead-valve engine. Overall gear ratios with principal Coventry Climax engine 4.70, 6.46, 10.41, 17.11, reverse 22.37:1, with synchromesh on top, third and second gears. Close-ratio gears also available. 15.32mph/1,000rpm in top gear.

Suspension and brakes: Ifs, transverse torsion-bars, twin trailing-arms, telescopic hydraulic dampers. Irs, transverse torsion-bars, twin trailing-arms, radius-arms, telescopic hydraulic dampers. Worm-and-sector steering. 11 × 2.25in front and rear brakes; 11 × 1.75in on later cars. 5.00—15in or 5.60—15in tyres on 4.5in rims. Centre-lock wire-spoke wheels.

Dimensions: Wheelbase 7ft 0in; front track 4ft 3in; rear track 4ft 4in. Length 11ft 6in; width 5ft 4in; height 4ft 0in. Fuel tank 8.75 galls. Unladen weight 1,455lb with Coventry Climax engine, 1,570lb with MGA engine.

Basic price: Kits, £950 (with Coventry Climax engine), £800 (with MGA engine), £695 (with Ford 105E engine), £660 (with Ford 100E engine).

Grantura Mark II — produced 1960 and 1961

Specifications as for Grantura Mark I except for:

Engine: Choice of BMC, Coventry Climax or Ford engines. Principal engine: BMC, MGA 1600 unit, 4-cyl, 75.39 × 88.9mm, 1,588cc, CR 8.3:1, 2 SU carbs, pushrod-operated overhead valve gear. 79.5bhp (net) at 5,600rpm. Maximum torque 87lb ft at 3,800rpm.

Alternative engines: Ford (overhead valve) 105E unit, Coventry Climax (overhead-camshaft) FWE unit; a few MGA 1500 engines of 1,489cc, 72bhp (net) at 5,500rpm, were also fitted.

Transmission: Axle ratio and gearbox depending on engine chosen. With MGA 1600 unit, axle ratio 4.3:1. Overall gear ratios 4.3, 5.908, 9.52, 15.652, reverse 20.468:1, with synchromesh on top, third and second gears.

17.0mph/1,000rpm in top gear. Optional axle ratios 4.1, 4.55, 4.875, 5.1:1. Optional close-ratio gears, or optional ZF four-speed gearbox.

Suspension and brakes: 11 × 1.75in drum brakes, front and rear. 5.60—15in tyres. Rack-and-pinion steering option on Coventry Climax-engined cars.

Basic price: Kits, £880 (with MGA engine), £1,045 (with Coventry Climax engine), £795 (with Ford 109E engine).

Grantura Mark IIA — produced 1961 and 1962

Specifications are for Grantura Mark II except for:

Engine: Most cars built with MGA 1600 Mark II engine, 4-cyl, 76.2 × 88.9mm, 1,622cc, CR 8.9:1, 2 SU carbs, pushrod-operated overhead valve gear, 86bhp (net) at 5,500rpm. Maximum torque 97lb ft at 4,000rpm. Early cars available with MGA 1,588cc engine, plus previous Ford and Coventry Climax engine options. Further alternative engine, Ford (overhead-valve) 109E of 1,340cc, 54bhp (net) at 4,900rpm.

Suspension and brakes: 11.25in front discs, 11 × 1.75in rear drums.

Grantura Mark III — produced 1962 to 1964

Engine: MGA 1600 Mark II engine to September 1963, MGB 1800 engine thereafter. Ford and Coventry Climax engine options listed, but very few cars built with those units.

MGA 1600 Mark II engine: 4-cyl, 76.2 × 88.9mm, 1,622cc, CR 8.9:1, 2 SU carbs, 86bhp (net) at 5,500rpm. Maximum torque 97lb ft at 4,000rpm.

MGB 1800 engine: 4-cyl, 80.26 × 88.9mm, 1,798cc, CR 8.8:1. 2 SU carbs, 95bhp (net) at 5,400rpm. Maximum torque 110lb ft at 3,000 rpm.

Transmission: Axle ratios to choice, 4.1, 4.55, 4.875, 5.1:1. Normally 4.55:1 with 1,622cc engine and overall ratios 4.55, 6.25, 10.07, 16.56, reverse 21.66:1. 16.1mph/1,000rpm. Normally 4.1:1 with 1,798cc engine and overall ratios 4.1, 5.633, 9.077, 14.924, reverse 19.516:1. 17.8mph/1,000rpm in top gear. Synchromesh on top, third and second gears. Optional overdrive on top and third gears: overall overdrive top gear ratio with 4.1 axle, 3.30:1, 22.1mph/1,000rpm in overdrive top gear.

Suspension and brakes: Ifs, wishbones, coil spring/telescopic damper units and anti-roll bar. Irs, wishbones and coil spring/telescopic damper units. Rack-and-pinion steering. 10.75in front disc brakes, 9 × 1.75in rear drums. Centre-lock wire-spoke wheels or steel-disc wheels with 4.5in rims. 5.60—15in tyres.

Dimensions: Wheelbase 7ft 1.5in; front track 4ft 3in; rear track 4ft 4in. Length 11ft 6in; width 5ft 4in; height 4ft 0in. Fuel tank 10 galls. Unladen weight 1,625lb with MGA or MGB engine.

Basic price: Kits, £862 (with MGA 1600 Mark II engine), £872 (with MGB 1800 engine).

Grantura 1800S — produced 1964 to 1966, and 'Mk IV' 1800S — produced 1966 to 1967
Specifications as for Grantura Mark III except for:
Engine: BMC MGB 1800 engine standardized with no options.
Transmission: Axle ratio 4.3:1 or 3.9:1, to choice. With 4.3:1 ratio, overall gear ratios 4.3, 5.908, 9.52, 15.652, reverse 20.468:1; optional overdrive on top and third gears, overall overdrive top ratio 3.45:1. 17.0mph/1,000rpm in direct top gear, 21.2mph/1,000rpm in overdrive top gear. With 3.91:1 ratio, overall gear ratios 3.91, 5.37, 8.66, 14.21, reverse 18.59:1; optional overdrive on top and third gears, overall overdrive top ratio 3.14:1. 18.7mph/1,000rpm in direct top gear, 23.3mph/1,000rpm in overdrive top gear.
Dimensions: Front track 4ft 4.5in; rear track 4ft 5.5in. Fuel tank (Mark IVS) 15 galls. Unladen weight (Mark IVS) 1,790lb.
Basic price: £872 at first, £927 from February 1965, £981 from June 1965, £988 from revival of production in Spring 1966.

Vixen SI — produced 1967 and 1968
Engine: Ford Cortina GT 1600 engine, 4-cyl, 80.98 × 77.62mm, 1,599cc, CR 9.0:1, two-choke Weber carb, 88bhp (net) at 5,400rpm. Maximum torque 96lb ft at 3,600rpm.**
Transmission: Ford all-synchromesh gearbox with axle ratio of 3.89:1. Overall gear ratios 3.89, 5.45, 7.84, 11.59, reverse 12.91:1. 18.8mph/1,000rpm in top gear.
**A few cars were fitted with MGB 1,798cc engine and BMC gearbox, left over from Grantura Mark IVS production.
Suspension and brakes: Ifs, wishbones, coil spring/telescopic damper units and anti-roll bar. Irs, wishbones and coil spring/telescopic damper units. Rack-and-pinion steering. 10.75in front disc brakes, 9 × 1.75in rear drums. Steel-disc or centre-lock wire-spoke wheels with 4.5in rims. 165—15in tyres.
Dimensions: Wheelbase 7ft 1.5in; front track 4ft 4.5in; rear track 4ft 5.5in. Length 11ft 6in; width 5ft 4in; height 4ft 0in. Fuel tank 15 galls. Unladen weight 1,735lb.
Basic price: £988 at first, £1,095 from April 1967.

Vixen S2 — produced 1968 to 1970
Specification as for Vixen S1 except for:
Engine: MGB engine option not available.
Brakes: With servo-assistance from 1969.
Dimensions: Wheelbase 7ft 6in; front track 4ft 5in; rear track 4ft 6in. Length 12ft 1in; width 5ft 4in; height 4ft 0in. Unladen weight 1,680lb.
Basic price: £1,095 at first, £1,150 from January 1969, £1,242 from May 1970.

Vixen S3 — produced 1970 to 1972
Specification as for Vixen S2 except for:
Engine: Ford power output now quoted as 86bhp (DIN) at 5,500rpm. Maximum torque 92lb ft (DIN) at 4,000rpm.
Wheels, bolt-on cast-alloy with 5.5in rims. Unladen weight 1,625lb.
Basic price: £1,245 at first, £1,295 from April 1971, £1,310 from July 1971.

1300 — produced 1971 and 1972
Specification as for Vixen S2 except for:
Engine: BL Triumph Spitfire unit, 4-cyl, 73.7 × 76mm, 1,296cc, CR 9.0:1, 2 SU carbs, 63bhp (DIN) at 6,000rpm. Maximum torque 69lb ft at 3,500rpm.
Transmission: BL Triumph Spitfire all-synchromesh gearbox. Axle ratio 3.89:1. Overall gear ratios 3.89, 5.41, 8.41, 13.65, reverse 15.51:1. 17.8mph/1,000rpm in top gear.
Suspension and brakes: no brake servo-assistance. Bolt-on cast-alloy road wheels with 5.5in rims.
Dimensions: Unladen weight 1,625lb.
Basic price: £1,245 at first, £1,355 from April 1972, £1,422 from July 1972.
Note: The last six 1300s were fitted with M-Series chassis — see below.

All the above TVRs had four-cylinder engines. The following cars fitted with the 1962-72 coil-spring chassis-frame were also produced:

Griffith 200 and Griffith 400 V8 — produced 1963 to 1965
Specification as for Grantura Mark III and 1800S except for:
Engine: USA Ford V-8 units in two states of tune. 195bhp unit: V-8-cyl, 101.6 × 72.9mm, 4,727cc, CR 9.0:1, four-choke downdraught Ford carb, 195bhp (gross). Maximum torque 282lb ft at 2,400rpm. 271bhp unit: CR 11.0:1, 271bhp (gross) at 6,500rpm. Maximum torque 314lb ft at 3,400rpm.
Transmission: Axle ratio 3.07:1. Overall gear ratios 3.07, 4.33, 5.46, 7.25, reverse 7.25:1. 25mph/1,000rpm in top gear. Synchromesh on all forward gears.
Suspension and brakes: Extra spring/damper units on rear suspension. Servo-assisted brakes. 185—15in tyres on 5.0in wheels. All cars built with centre-lock wire-spoke wheels.
Dimensions: Fuel tank 17 galls. Unladen weight 1,905lb.
Basic price: (Only sold in Britain during 1965) £1,342 at first, £1,400 from June 1965.

Tuscan V8 — produced in 1967
Specification as for Grantura Mark III except for:
Engine: USA Ford V-8 units as for Griffith 200/400 models.
Transmission: Ford gearbox as for Griffith 200/400 models.
Suspension, dimensions and weight: As for Griffith 400 model, except fuel tank 15 galls.
Basic price: £1,599, or £1,922 as SE model with 271bhp (gross) engine.

Tuscan V8 SE — long wheelbase — produced 1967 and 1968
Specifications as for Griffith 400 and Tuscan V8 models except for:
Suspension and brakes: Wire wheels with 6.0in rim widths.
Dimensions: Wheelbase 7ft 6in. Length 12ft 1in. Unladen weight 2,240lb.
Basic price: £1,922.

Tuscan V8 SE — long-wheelbase/wide-body — produced 1968 to 1970
Specifications as for Griffith 400 and Tuscan V8 models except for:

Suspension and brakes: Wire wheels with 6.0in rim widths.
Dimensions: Wheelbase 7ft 6in. Length 12ft 2in; width 5ft 8in.
Basic price: Not quoted — only three cars sold in Britain.

Tuscan V6 — produced 1969 to 1971
Specifications as for Vixen S2/S3 except for:
Engine: British Ford unit, V-6-cyl, 93.66 × 72.4mm, 2,994cc, CR 8.9:1, two-choke Weber carb, 128bhp (DIN) at 4,750rpm. Maximum torque 173lb ft at 3,000rpm.
Transmission: Ford all-synchromesh gearbox. Axle ratio (early cars) 3.31:1. Overall gear ratios 3.31, 4.67, 7.33, 10.47, reverse 11.08:1. Optional overdrive on top and third gears; overall ratio in overdrive top 2.72:1. 22.0mph/1,000rpm in direct top gear, 26.9mph/1,000rpm in overdrive top gear. Axle ratio (later cars) 3.54:1. Overall gear ratios 3.54, 5.00, 7.84, 11.20, reverse 11.84:1. 20.0mph/1,000rpm in top gear.
Dimensions: Unladen weight 2,000lb.
Basic price: £1,492 at first, £1,558 from May 1970, £1,595 from April 1971.

2500 — produced 1971 and 1972
Specifications as for Vixen S2/S3 except for:
Engine: Triumph TR6 (federal-tune) engine, 6-cyl, 74.7 × 95mm, 2,498cc, CR 8.5:1, 2 Zenith-Stromberg carbs, 106bhp (net) at 4,900rpm. Maximum torque 133lb ft at 3,000rpm.
Transmission: Triumph rear axle and gearbox. Axle ratio 3.45:1. All-synchromesh gearbox with optional overdrive on top and third gears. Overall gear ratios (o/d 2.83), 3.45, 4.59, 6.94, 10.83, reverse 11.11 to 21.1mph/1,000rpm in direct top gear, 25.7mph/1,000rpm in overdrive top gear.
Dimensions: Unladen weight 1,960lb.
Basic price: £1,500 at first, £1,430 from October 1971, £1,560 from May 1972, £1,638 from August 1972.
Note: The last series of 2500s, built in the spring and summer of 1972, had M-Type chassis — see below.
From the spring of 1972, a new basic chassis-frame, known as the M-Type chassis, was standardized for all new TVRs. The M-Type range consisted of 2500M, 1600M, 3000M, Taimar and Convertible derivatives:

2500M — produced 1972 to 1977
Engine: Triumph TR6 (federal-tune) unit, 6-cyl, 74.7 × 95mm, 2,498cc, CR 7.75:1 (from 1974, CR 7.5:1), 2 Zenith-Stromberg carbs, 106bhp (net) at 4,900rpm. Maximum torque 133lb ft at 3,000rpm.
Transmission: Triumph rear axle and gearbox. Axle ratio 3.45:1. All-synchromesh gearbox with optional overdrive on top and third gears. Overall gear ratios (o/d 2.83), 3.45, 4.59, 6.94, 10.83, reverse 11.11:1. 21.1mph/1,000rpm in direct top gear, 25.7mph/1,000rpm in overdrive top gear.
Suspension and brakes: Ifs, wishbones, coil spring/telescopic damper units and anti-roll bar. Irs, wishbones, coil spring/telescopic damper units. Rack-and-pinion steering. 10.9in front disc brakes, 9 × 1.75in rear drum brakes,

with vacuum servo assistance. Cast-alloy bolt-on disc wheels with 5.5in rims and 165—15in tyres; from Autumn 1973, 6.0in wheel rims and 185HR—14in tyres.
Dimensions: Wheelbase 7ft 6in; front track 4ft 5.75in; rear track 4ft 5.75in. Length 12ft 10in; width 5ft 4in; height 4ft 0in. Fuel tank 12 galls. Unladen weight 2,240lb.
Basic price: £1,560 at first, £1,695 when into production in Spring 1972, £1,779 from August 1972. Discontinued in Britain in May 1973.

Vixen S4 — produced in 1972 and 1973
Specifications as for 2500M except for:
Engine: Ford 1600GT overhead-valve unit, 4-cyl, 80.98 × 77.62mm, 1,599cc, CR 9.0:1, two-choke Weber carb, 86bhp (DIN) at 5,500rpm. Maximum torque 92lb ft at 4,000rpm.
Transmission: Ford all-synchromesh gearbox. Axle ratio 3.89:1. Overall gear ratios 3.89, 5.57, 8.02, 11.34, reverse 12.90:1. 18.8mph/1,000rpm in top gear.
Dimensions: Length 12ft 1in. Unladen weight 1,625lb.
Basic price: £1,425 at first, £1,496 from August 1972.

1600M — produced 1972 to 1973, then 1975 to 1977
Specifications as for 2500M except for:
Engine: Ford 1600GT overhead-valve unit, 4-cyl, 80.98 × 77.62mm, 1,599cc, CR 9.0:1, two-choke Weber carb, 86bhp (DIN) at 5,500rpm. Maximum torque 92lb ft at 4,000rpm.
Transmission: Ford all-synchromesh gearbox. Axle ratio 3.89:1. Overall gear ratios 3.89, 5.57, 8.02, 11.34, reverse 12.90:1. 18.8mph/1,000rpm in top gear.
Dimensions: Unladen weight 1,970lb.
Basic price: £1,560 at first, £1,638 in August 1972 and 1973, £2,200 when re-introduced in 1975, rising rapidly to £2,975 by Autumn 1976.

3000M — produced 1972 to 1979
Specifications as for 2500M except for:
Engine: British Ford unit, V-6-cyl, 93.66 × 72.4mm, 2,994cc, CR 8.9:1, two-choke Weber carb, 138bhp (DIN) at 5,000rpm. Maximum torque 174lb ft at 3,000rpm.
Transmission: Ford all-synchromesh gearbox. Axle ratio 3.45:1. Overall gear ratios 3.45, 4.86, 6.72, 10.90, reverse 11.56:1. 21.6mph/1,000rpm in top gear. Overdrive not available until Autumn 1975.
Dimensions: Unladen weight 2,240lb.
Basic price: £1,795 in mid-1972, rising to £6,417 when discontinued in 1980.

Taimar — produced 1976 to 1979
Specifications as for 3000M except for hatchback body and:
Engine: 142bhp (DIN) at 5,000rpm.
Dimensions: Unladen weight 2,260lb.
Basic price: £4,260 in Autumn 1976, rising to £7,211 when discontinued in 1980.

Convertible — produced 1978 and 1979

Specifications as for 3000M except for convertible body and:
Engine: 142bhp (DIN) at 5,000rpm.
Dimensions: Height 3ft 9in. Unladen weight 2,420lb.
Basic price: £5,462 in mid-1978, rising to £7,007 when discontinued in 1980.

Note: From 1976 to 1980, on 3000M, Taimar and Convertible models, a turbocharged engine option was available. Specification differences were as follows:
Engine: CR 8.0:1, two-choke Weber carburettor with Broadspeed/Holset or AiResearch turbocharger installation. 230bhp (DIN) at 5,500rpm. Maximum torque 273lb ft at 3,500rpm.
Transmission: Axle ratio 3.31:1. Overall gear ratios 3.31, 4.67, 6.45, 10.46, reverse 11.09:1. 21.7mph/1,000rpm in top gear. 195/70VR — 14in tyres.
Basic price: Extra charge for installation £2,490 in spring 1976, rising to £3,210 by 1980.

At the end of 1979, the M-Series chassis was discontinued and TVR introduced their first all-new chassis and bodyshell since the late-1950s. This was the Tasmin, announced in two-seater fixed-head form in January 1980 and later available in other derivatives:

Tasmin S1 (two-seater coupe) — produced 1980 and 1981

Engine: German Ford unit, V-6 cyl, 93 × 68.5mm, 2,792cc; CR 9.2:1, Bosch K-Jetronic fuel injection. 160bhp (DIN) at 5,700rpm. Maximum torque 162lb ft at 4,300rpm.
Transmission: Ford all-synchromesh gearbox, or Ford automatic transmission. Axle ratio 3.07:1. Overall gear ratios (manual transmission) 3.07, 4.33, 5.96, 9.70, reverse 10.28:1. Overall gear ratios (automatic transmission) 3.07, 4.53, 7.60, reverse 6.48:1. 22.2mph/1,000rpm in top gear.
Suspension and brakes: Ifs, coil springs, wishbones, anti-roll bar, telescopic dampers. Irs, trailing links, transverse links, fixed-length drive-shafts, combined coil spring/telescopic damper units. Rack-and-pinion steering. 10.6in front disc brakes, 10.9in rear discs, with vacuum-servo assistance. Bolt-on cast-alloy disc wheels with 7.0in rims. 205/60VR — 14in tyres.
Dimensions: Wheelbase 7ft 10in; front track 4ft 8.5in; rear track 4ft 8.7in. Length 13ft 2in; width 5ft 8in; height 3ft 11in. Fuel tank 14 galls. Unladen weight 2,365lb.
Basic price: £10,274 in Spring 1980 with manual transmission, automatic transmission £400 (basic) extra. £11,096 from May 1981.

Tasmin S2 Coupe — produced 1981 to 1985

(Renamed 280i Coupe in 1983)
1981 specification, as for Tasmin S1 Coupe except for:

Length 13ft 5in. Engine later re-rated by Ford to 150bhp (DIN) at 5,700rpm.
From October 1982: Optional Ford five-speed all-synchromesh gearbox, with axle ratio of 3.54:1. Overall gear ratios 2.90, 3.54, 4.53, 6.37, 11.89, reverse 11.91:1. 24.5mph/1000rpm in top (fifth) gear. Other options included automatic transmission, power-assisted steering and air-conditioning.
Basic price: £12,855 from May 1986, total price £16,015.
Note: USA-market version went on sale from Spring 1984, with 145bhp at 5,700rpm, overall length 13ft 7in and unladen weight approx 2,700lb.

Tasmin Convertible — produced 1980 to 1987

(Renamed 280i Convertible in 1983)
1981 specification as for Tasmin coupe except for convertible body style:
Length 13ft 2in. Engine later re-rated to 150bhp as S2 Coupe.
From October 1982: Optional Ford five-speed all-synchromesh gearbox, automatic transmission, power-assisted steering and air-conditioning, details as Coupe S2.
Basic price: £12,200 from May 1986, total price £15,200.
Note: USA-market version went on sale from Spring 1983 with 145bhp at 5,700rpm and overall length of 13ft 4in. This car became 'Series II' from Spring 1985 with styling and equipment changes.

Tasmin +2 — produced 1981 to 1985

Specification and all updating changes as for the Tasmin S2 Coupe except for +2 seating.
Basic price: £11,077 in Autumn 1980, automatic transmission £400 (basic) extra. Last quoted price £12,690 in 1985.

Tasmin 200 Coupe — produced 1981 to 1984

Specification as for 2.8-litre Tasmin S2 Coupe except for:
Engine: Ford overhead-cam unit, 4-cyl, 90.8 × 76.95mm, 1,993cc, CR 9.2:1, two-choke Weber carb, 101bhp (DIN) at 5,200rpm. Maximum torque 112lb ft at 3,500rpm.
Transmission: Axle ratio 3.44:1. Overall gear ratios 3.44, 4.71, 6.78, 12.56, reverse 12.59:1. 19.1mph/1,000rpm in top gear. No automatic transmission option.
Suspension: 6.0in wheel rims, 195/60HR — 14in tyres.
Dimensions: Unladen weight 2,138lb.
Basic price: £8,015 on announcement in December 1981.

Tasmin 200 Convertible — produced 1981 to 1984

Specification as for 2.8-litre Tasmin Convertible except for mechanical details as for 200 Coupe.
Basic price: £7,934 on announcement in December 1981.

350i Convertible — produced 1983 to 1985

Specification as for Tasmin/280i Convertible except for:
Engine: Rover overhead-valve unit, V-8-cyl, 88.9 × 71.12mm, 3,528cc, CR

9.75:1, Lucas fuel injection. 190bhp (DIN) at 5,280rpm. Maximum torque 220lb ft at 4,000rpm.
Transmission: Rover all-synchromesh gearbox, or GM automatic transmission. Axle ratio 3.54:1. Overall gear ratios (manual transmission) 2.80, 3.54, 4.96, 7.40, 11.75, reverse 12.14:1. 25.4mph/1,000rpm in top (fifth) gear. Overall gear ratios (automatic transmission) 3.54, 5.24, 8.50, reverse 6.80. 20.1mph/1,000rpm in top gear.
Suspension: 7.0in wheel rims. 205/60VR — 15in tyres.
Dimensions: Height 3ft 11.5in. Unladen weight 2,536lb.
Basic price: £11,880 on announcement in Autumn 1983.
Automatic transmission £417 (basic), power-assisted steering £265 (basic) and air-conditioning for £534 (basic) extra.

350i Convertible Series 2 — produced 1985 to date
Specification as for Series I model except for:
Engine: 197bhp (DIN) at 5,280rpm.
Basic price: £13,625 from May 1986.

350i Coupe — produced 1983 to date
Specification as for Tasmin/280i S2 Coupe except for mechanical details as for 350i Convertible.

350i +2 Coupe — produced 1983 and 1984
Specification as for Tasmin/280i +2 Coupe except for mechanical details as for 350i Convertible.

390SE Convertible — produced 1984 to date
Sold as an Option Package on the 350i Convertible. Same specification except for:
Engine: 93.5 × 71.12mm, 3,905cc, CR 10.5:1, 275bhp (DIN) at 5,500rpm. Maximum torque 270lb ft at 3,500rpm.
Transmission: Limited-slip differential as standard.
Suspension: 225/50VR — 15in, later 225/60VR — 15in, tyres.
Price: Always priced as a conversion on top of 350i prices. From May 1986 *total* extra UK cost was £3,810.
Note: To special customer order, a few cars were fitted with 4.2-litre engine, as to be used in 420SEAC model.

Supplement
In almost every case the original source of TVR engines and gearboxes is quite clear. In the case of final-drive/differential units, however, there may be more difficulty in identifying the sources. These can be identified as followed:

BMC B-Series differentials
Grantura Mark I
Grantura Mark II
Grantura Mark IIA
Grantura 1800S
Vixen S1
Griffith 200

Triumph Vitesse/GT6 differentials
Vixen S2
Vixen S3
Vixen S4
1300
1600M

Triumph TR6 differentials
2500
2500M
3000M (1972 to 1976/7)
Taimar (1976 to early-1977)

Salisbury 4HU-type differentials
Griffith 400
Tuscan V8
Tuscan V6
3000M (from Chassis Number 3919, March 1977)
Taimar (from Chassis Number 3919, March 1977)
Convertible
Turbo derivatives
Tasmin family

APPENDIX C

Chassis Number sequences

Everyone on the staff of TVR has given me every possible assistance in compiling the table of Chassis Number sequences which follows. However, I should explain that existing records held by TVR only originate with the rebirth of the company in the winter of 1965-6 and that earlier information has been supplied from the memory of that remarkable TVR staff man, Stan Kilcoyne.

Once TVR was started up again by the Lilley family, an entirely new sequence of Chassis Numbers was adopted. With the exception of the Ford V-8-engined cars (Griffith and Tuscan V-8-types), which had their own separate sequences, all other TVRs built from 1966 to 1979 took up the appropriate number issued when that particular car was built. The sequence started from . . . 001 in February 1966 and ended at . . . 4970 in December 1979, with a single hiccup — the last Vixen Series 1 was VX233, while the first Vixen Series 2 which followed it was VX1234/F — in other words there was a jump of 1,000 numbers at that point, in October 1968.

What this means is that not all cars built between — say — LVX 1283/6 and LVX 2134/6 were Tuscan V6 models, but that all Tuscan V6s were contained inside the spread of these numbers. In case any TVR owner suspects that the car he buys is not what it seems, he should be happy to know that the record books have been preserved at Blackpool, and it was these which I consulted in preparing the table:

Model	Years Built	Engine	Chassis Numbers
Grantura Mk I	1958-1960	MGA/MGB	7B
Grantura Mk II	1960-1961	Coventry Climax	7C — 001 onwards
Grantura Mk IIA	1961-1962	Ford	7F
Grantura Mk III	1962-1964	MGA/MGB	18-001 onwards
Grantura 1800S	1964-1966	MGB	
Griffith 200	1963-1964		200-001 onwards
Griffith 400	1964-1965	Ford V8	400-001 onwards
Griffith 400	1965		200/GB/5001 onwards

Following rebirth under the management of the Lilley family:

Grantura 1800S	1966	MGB	18/001-18/044
Grantura 'Mk IV' 1800S	1966-1967	MGB	18/027-18/116
Vixen S1	1967-1968	Ford 1600	VX117-VX233
Vixen S2	1968-1970	Ford 1600	LVX1234/F-LVX1736/4
Vixen S3	1970-1972	Ford 1600	LVX1737/4-LVX2239/4
Vixen S4	1972-1973	Ford 1600	2271/4-2597/4
Griffith	1966-1967	Ford V8	200-001 — 200-010
Tuscan V8	1967	Ford V8	200-011 to 015, 017 to 020, 022 to 040
Tuscan V8 lwb	1967-1968	Ford V8	LWB-001 to LWB-024
Tuscan V6	1969-1971	Ford V6 3.0	LVX1283/6-LVX2134/6
Tuscan V8 (wide body)	1968-1970	Ford V8	MAL001-MAL021
2500	1970-1972	Triumph 2500	1745/6T-2703/T
1300	1971-1973	Triumph 1300	1992/S-2557/4S
2500M	1972-1977	Triumph 2500	2090T, then 2240TM-4094TM
1600M	1972-1973 and 1975-1977	Ford 1600	2288FM-2623FM, then 3384FM-3938FM
3000M	1972-1979	Ford V6 3.0	2410FM-4940FM
Taimar	1976-1979	Ford V6 3.0	3838FM-4966FM
Convertible	1978-1979	Ford V6 3.0	4286FM-4968FM

A new sequence of chassis identification was then adopted for the new Tasmin series:

Tasmin Coupe S1	1979 to 1981	Ford V6 2.8	FH5001FI to 5196FI
Tasmin Convertible	1980 onwards	Ford V6 2.8	DH5098FI onwards
Tasmin +2 Coupe	1980 onwards	Ford V6 2.8	FH5113FI2 onwards
Tasmin Coupe S2	1981 onwards	Ford V6 2.8	FH5211FIT onwards

| Tasmin 200s | 1981 to 1984 | Ford 2000 | ...... 2L suffix |
| 350i/390SE | 1983 onwards | Rover V8 3.5/3.9 | ......RI suffix |

This chassis number sequence was abandoned, at DH6040FI, in March, 1985. From that date, 'Euro-rationalized' Vehicle Identification Numbers (VIN Nos) were adopted. The first of the new-style VINs was:

TV9RF28P4FBDH1280RI

— where the last eight digits (DH1280RI) coincided with the old-style chassis sequence.

This sequence was changed from mid-1985, from:

SA9DH28PXFB019433

Each of the digits means the following:

S } Made in the UK.
A } Less than 500 vehicles per annum.
9 }

D } Description of body.   DH = drop-head, FH = fixed-head.
H } Weight class B (3,001-4,000lb GVW).

2 } Engine size.   28 = Ford 2.8 litre.
8 }   35 = Rover 3.5 litre.

P } Fuel.   P = Petrol or gasoline.

X } VIN Verification check digit.

F } Manufacturing year.   F = 1985, G = 1986, H = 1987.

B } Manufacturing plant.   B = Blackpool.

0 } International code, designating TVR 280i & 350i fixed-
1 } head & drop-head. TVR Engineering Limited, Bristol
9 } Avenue, Blackpool, Lancs, FY2 0JF.

4 }
3 } Sequential build number.
3 }

Notes:

1. In the case of early Granturas, the first letter in the sequence pinpoints the engine — B for BMC (MG) type, C for Coventry Climax and F for Ford, of whatever type.
2. MGB-engined cars are pinpointed by the prefix '18' in the Chassis Number sequence.
3. Series 1 Vixens are identified by the prefix 'VX'. When the Vixen Series 2 was introduced, the wheelbase was increased, so it was logical that the

prefix should be 'LVX'. The Tuscan V6 and the 2500 model both used the same basic chassis, and the V6 also adopted the 'LVX' prefix.
4. Progressively, from the introduction of the Vixen Series 2, the chassis prefixes were phased out and a series of suffixes were brought in in their place:
Vixen 2, 3 and 4 models carried the suffix . . . /4 (early cars . . . /F)
Tuscan V6 models carried the suffix . . . /6
2500 models carried the suffix . . . /6T, which was later reduced to . . . /T
1300 models carried the suffix . . . /S (or . . . /4S)
5. All cars based on the M-Series chassis (except the 1971 prototype 2500M) used numbers ending with . . . M, as follows:
2500M models carried the suffix . . . TM
1600M models carried the suffix . . . FM
3000M models carried the suffix . . . FM
Taimar models carried the suffix . . . FM
Convertible models carried the suffix . . . FM
6. A search of the chassis records confirms that almost all Convertibles had even-number Chassis Numbers. However, the occasional 3000M or Taimar also slipped into this sequence. In general, however, from early-1978, the Convertible took over all even numbers from 4286FM. Because of the imbalance caused by the above arrangement, the last odd number to be issued was 4699FM, and this was, in fact, a Convertible!
7. There was a clear cut-off point between pre-M, and M-Series chassis. The last pre-M chassis was 2239 (a Series 3 Vixen), and the first M-Series chassis was 2240TM (a 2500M); there was no overlap.
8. Tasmin S2 Coupe numbering changed almost immediately after release. From Chassis Number 5232, a complete identification became 2FH5232FI.
9. Identification of the Turbos — turbocharged engines supplied on 3000M, Taimar and Convertible bases — is considered interesting enough for all the cars to be listed individually. This is done below.
10. An entirely new sequence was adopted for the Tasmin models. Numbers start at 5001. The prefix FH refers to a fixed-head car (2-seat or 2+2-seat), while DH refers to the drop-head or Convertible Tasmin. The suffix FI refers to the fuel-injected Ford engine; the +2 model has a number 2 after the FI — *viz*, FI2.
11. Following the disastrous fire at the Bristol Avenue works, on January 3, 1975, there was a considerable hiatus before production could begin again. The first 'post-fire' car to be completed — a 3000M — carried Chassis Number 3380FM.
12. The move to Bristol Avenue took place over Christmas 1970. The first car to be completed at the new premises carried Chassis Number LVX 1806/6 and was a Tuscan V6.
13. After the introduction of the M-Series chassis in April 1972, some Vixen, 1300 and 2500 models were built with M-Series chassis and old-style bodies. Details were as follows:

Vixen S4 — 23 cars from 2271/4 to 2597/4

1300 — 6 cars, culminating in 2557/4S

2500 — 96 cars from 2258T to 2703T

The exclusive Turbo model

Between September 1975 and December 1979, a total of 63 cars were built with turbocharged 3-litre engines. Their Chassis Numbers and body styles were as follows:

3463	3000M	4125	Taimar	4471	Taimar
3569	3000M	4170	3000M	4488	Convertible
3587	3000M	4197	Taimar	4537	Taimar
3597	3000M	4207	Taimar	4550	Convertible
3604	3000M	4243	Taimar	4565	Taimar
3606	3000M	4244	3000M	4566	3000M
3620	3000M	4254	3000M	4567	Taimar
3789	3000M	4279	Taimar	4571	Taimar
3815	3000M	4298	3000M	4608	3000M
3837	Taimar	4311	Taimar	4647	Taimar
3840	Taimar	4313	Taimar	4649	Taimar

3841	3000M	4325	Taimar	4661	Taimar
3844	Taimar	4327	Taimar	4673	Taimar
3850	Taimar	4332	3000M	4697	Convertible
3853	Taimar	4338	3000M	4704	Convertible
3957	Taimar	4354	Convertible	4746	Convertible
3961	Taimar	4362	Convertible	4768	Convertible
3965	Taimar	4404	Convertible	4800	3000M
3999	Taimar	4422	Convertible	4808	Convertible
4015	Taimar	4423	Taimar	4938	3000M
4105	Taimar	4468	Convertible	4970	Convertible

Of the 63 cars, 20 were 3000Ms, 30 were Taimars and 13 were Convertibles.

Chassis Numbers 3850, 4298, 4423 and 4647 were left-hand drive, all others being right-hand drive.

There were four 'SE' or Special Equipment Turbos — Chassis Numbers 4327, 4537, 4649 and 4768.

APPENDIX D

Production and deliveries

Two factors make it difficult to present a detailed and entirely accurate summary of TVR production from the time when series production of Granturas began in 1958 to the present day. One is that the tempestuous commercial history which was normal at TVR throughout the 1958-1965 period means that the present management does not have any of the old records. The other is that TVR Engineering Ltd has latterly detailed its chassis records not by the date at which a particular car was completed and delivered, but by the date when the production works *order* was issued to the workshops.

What I have tried to do, therefore, is to give full and accurate production totals for each different and identifiable model and — wherever possible — to break this down into the number of cars *ordered into production* in any particular calendar year.

Annual production figures

TVR became members of the Society of Motor Manufacturers and Traders in 1967, and the SMM & T have been able to provide me with the following figures for the calendar years 1970 to 1985:

Year	Total production	Home market	Export market
1970	284	190	94
1971	360	181	179
1972	388	220	168
1973	388	101	287
1974	421	36	385
1975	132*	91	41
1976	333	186	147
1977	366	213	153
1978	310	164	146
1979	308	168	140
1980	144**	133	11
1981	164	146	18
1982	121	109	12
1983	291	192	99
1984	397	162	235
1985	472	161	311

* As a result of the fire of January 1975
** As a result of the major model changeover to Tasmin.

Total production of each model

For TVR models built before the end of 1965 the totals quoted are approximations. Thereafter, it has been possible to provide exact figures:

Model	Total production	Comments
Grantura Mk I	100	
Grantura Mk II	400 approx.	
Grantura Mk IIA		
Grantura Mk III	90 approx.	
Grantura 1800S	90 approx.	
Griffith	300 approx.	(All but approx. 20 exported)

From the beginning of 1966, under the control of the Lilley family:

Model	Total production	Comments
Grantura 1800S	38	Including 7 right-hand drive cars, all built in 1966
Grantura 'Mk IV' 1800S	78	40 LHD, 38 RHD, built in 1966 and 1967
Griffith	10	4 RHD, 6 LHD, built in 1966 and 1967
Vixen S1	117	12 with MGB engine, 105 with Ford 1600GT engine
Vixen S2	438	47 delivered in 1968 209 delivered in 1969 182 delivered in 1970
Vixen S3	168	50 delivered in 1970 97 delivered in 1971 21 delivered in 1972
Vixen S4	23	22 ordered in 1972 1 ordered in 1973
Tuscan V8	28	4 RHD, 24 LHD, all built in 1967
Tuscan V8 lwb	24	12 each, RHD and LHD, 1967 and 1968
Tuscan V8 (wide-body)	21	All but two with LHD, built 1968 to 1970
Tuscan V6	101	32 delivered in 1969 50 delivered in 1970 19 delivered in 1971
2500	385	8 ordered in 1970 237 ordered in 1971 44 ordered in 1972 — the above 289 cars having old-type (Vixen-style) chassis. Plus a further 96 more cars with M-Type chassis and old-style bodies: 95 ordered in 1972 1 ordered in 1973

Model	Total production	Comments
		All annual figures quoted below are for cars *annually ordered into production:*
1300	15	9 with old-style (Vixen) chassis 6 with M-Type chassis, all but the last car with old-style bodies
2500M	947	1 in 1971 112 in 1972 263 in 1973 372 in 1974 20 in 1975 103 in 1976 76 in 1977
1600M	148	57 in 1972 11 in 1973 — in 1974 50 in 1975 29 in 1976 1 in 1977
3000M	654	28 in 1972 120 in 1973 49 in 1974 84 in 1975 161 in 1976 132 in 1977 42 in 1978 38 in 1979
Taimar	395	15 in 1976 155 in 1977 125 in 1978 100 in 1979
Convertible	258	129 in 1978 129 in 1979
3000M Turbo	20	1 in 1975 9 in 1976 3 in 1977 5 in 1978 2 in 1979
Taimar Turbo	30	5 in 1976 7 in 1977 10 in 1978 8 in 1979
Convertible Turbo	13	7 in 1978 6 in 1979
Tasmin S1 Coupe	118	6 in 1979 103 in 1980 9 in 1981

Model	Total production	Comments
Tasmin Convertible***	812	25 in 1980
		93 in 1981
		54 in 1982
		92 in 1983
		174 in 1984
		239 in 1985
		135 in 1986
Tasmin +2 Coupe	47	14 in 1980
		27 in 1981
		1 in 1982
		3 in 1983
		2 in 1985
Tasmin S2 Coupe***	136	23 in 1981
		35 in 1982
		26 in 1983
		49 in 1984
		3 in 1985
Tasmin 200 Coupe	16	1 in 1981
		9 in 1982
		5 in 1983
		1 in 1984
Tasmin 200 Convertible	45	7 in 1981
		19 in 1982
		13 in 1983
		6 in 1984

Model	Total production	Comments
350i Convertible***	417	50 in 1983
		88 in 1984
		143 in 1985
		136 in 1986
350i Coupe***	36	10 in 1983
		11 in 1984
		9 in 1985
		6 in 1986
350i +2 Coupe	6	5 in 1983
		1 in 1984
390SE Convertible*** (includes some cars with 420 engines)	33	5 in 1984
		13 in 1985
		15 in 1986

*** Tasmin-family figures are taken up to August 31, 1986. At the time of writing, production of all models is going ahead at the rate of about 10 cars every week. Note: The Tasmin was renamed 280i from 1983.

Summary of production statistics:
Various managements up to the end of 1965 built about 980 TVRs. From the beginning of 1966, TVR Engineering Ltd built 1,445 cars with pre-M-Series body styles, followed by 2,466 cars of M-Series derivation. Of all the TVRs built since 1958, only 63 have had turbocharged engines, and only about 385 have had Ford V-8 engines.

Although Martin Lilley never noticed it, the 5,000th TVR car was probably built towards the end of 1980, soon after the Tasmin Convertible and +2 derivatives were launched.

APPENDIX E

How fast? How economical? How heavy? Performance figures for all TVRs

Assembling accurate and impartial sets of performance figures for TVRs has been fascinating, not only for the discovery of what they reveal, but because there are so many different models to compare, one with the other, over the years.

However, so that I could include performance data for as many models as possible, I have had to relax my rule which was rigidly applied to previous *Collector's Guides*. Even though they managed to test a good many TVRs between 1961 and 1980, *Autocar* never got their hands on an MG-engined Grantura, or either of the Tuscans (V6 or V8). It would have been wrong not to include some perfectly good statistics for these interesting cars, so I turned to *Motor,* who did test these cars.

I should emphasize, however, that *Motor's* testing methods differed slightly from those of *Autocar* until the end of the 1960s, when they acquired a fifth wheel, so there may be one or two slight inconsistencies in the figures quoted.

During the 1970s, the authoritative American magazine, *Road & Track,* tested several TVRs, and their figures for the 2500, 2500M, Convertible and Tuscan V8 are also included. I should point out, however, that a happy quirk in USA 'federal' regulations at the end of the 1970s allowed TVR to send in supplies of their 3-litre Ford V-6-engined cars with modifications done locally by Olsen Laboratories of California.

I am very disappointed not to be able to include figures for the most powerful Griffith model, as it does not appear to have been tested by any of the magazines whose methods I trust implicitly. However, *Motor's* Tuscan V8 of 1967 was effectively the same car as the Griffith 400 except that it was somewhat heavier, and was therefore not quite as shatteringly fast in acceleration through the gears.

Both *Motor's* Tuscans were given 'estimated' maximum speeds, the reason given (in each case) being that the magazine had not journeyed to the Continent to find a limit-free motor road on which to establish the true top speed. In the case of the V6, the car would have been over-revving in direct top at this speed, or pulling just 4,650 rpm in overdrive top. In the case of the V8, the 4.7-litre engine would have been turning over at 6,250 rpm (and maximum power was developed at 6,000 rpm).

Four-cylinder cars: There are few surprises in the comparison between models, but they confirm the fact that cars built after the establishment of the Lilley regime were no less lively, even though they were rather more heavy. For sure, the MGB engine/gearbox assembly must have been considerably heavier than the Ford power train, as a comparison between the Grantura Mark IVS and the Vixen S2 shows, while it is also quite clear that the adoption of the M-Series frame and body was responsible for another considerable increase in weight.

Six-cylinder and V-8 cars: As you might expect, there was very little difference in the performance of any of the 3-litre (British) Ford V-6-engined cars, and the latest 2.8-litre (German) Ford-engined Tasmin is not only faster than any of the normally aspirated 3-litre cars through the gears, but has better aerodynamics and a higher top speed.

Nothing more than a line of exclamation marks is needed to describe the performance of the Turbo-engined Convertible which *Autocar* tested in 1979 (no wonder their test sub-heading was 'Machismo lives . . .'). A figure-by-figure comparison with *Motor's* Tuscan V8 is very interesting, for the 230 bhp (DIN) Turbo was facing the 271 bhp (gross) Tuscan V8. The lesson is that the bigger 4.7-litre engine of the Tuscan V8 had more torque, but that the 3.0-litre Turbo engine had rather more high-speed urge. Since both rushed up to 100 mph in less than 15 seconds (a V-12 Jaguar E-Type tested by *Autocar,* incidentally, took 15.4 seconds) and both recorded between 16 and 18 mpg fuel consumption, you 'paid yer money and took yer choice'. (For status, refinement and better engineering, mine would be the Turbo.)

'Federalized' USA-market cars: The first thing to note is that the car tested by *Road & Track* in January 1973 was placarded as a 2500M, but actually had the old-type bodyshell and therefore counts as one of the last of the 2500s. The second is that the maximum speed of the 1970-type Tuscan V8 (which had the short-run, widened, bodyshell which was effectively the forerunner of the M-Series style) was restricted by the gearing and the valve-float limit (5,200 rpm) of the non-standard 4,949-cc Ford engine fitted to the test car. Incidentally, I simply cannot believe that the V8 was producing its 220 bhp (gross) for the performance figures are very little better than those quoted eight years later for the 135-bhp (DIN) 3-litre Convertible.

Tasmin-family cars: *Autocar* figures for three of the 1980s derivatives are included in the table. As far as I know, the Tasmin 200 (2-litre Ford 4-cylinder engine) has never been road-tested.

	Grantura IIA 1588cc 4-cyl MG	Grantura IIA 1216cc 4-cyl C-C	Grantura 1800S 1798cc 4-cyl MG	Vixen S2 1599cc 4-cyl Ford	1600M 1599cc 4-cyl Ford	Tuscan V6 2994cc 6-cyl Ford	3000M 2994cc 6-cyl Ford	Tasmin S1 2792cc 6-cyl Ford
Mean maximum speed (mph)	98	101	108	109	105	125*	121	130
Acceleration (sec)								
0-30 mph	4.4	4.2	4.4	3.6	3.2	2.6	2.5	3.2
0-40 mph	5.9	6.0	6.3	5.1	4.9	3.8	4.0	4.7
0-50 mph	9.3	8.2	8.4	7.4	7.2	6.0	5.8	6.4
0-60 mph	12.0	10.8	10.9	10.5	10.4	8.3	7.7	8.2
0-70 mph	17.2	15.2	14.3	14.0	14.3	11.1	10.6	10.3
0-80 mph	23.7	20.7	18.9	18.8	19.6	14.3	14.0	13.3
0-90 mph	–	27.8	25.5	26.4	27.8	18.7	18.8	16.8
0-100 mph	–	–	36.8	41.7	40.7	24.8	25.6	23.2
0-110 mph	–	–	–	–	–	33.5	37.0	32.5
0-120 mph	–	–	–	–	–	–	–	–
0-130 mph	–	–	–	–	–	–	–	–
Standing ¼-mile (sec)	19.0	18.3	18.0	17.2	17.6	16.2	16.0	16.4
Direct top gear (sec)								
10-30 mph	9.8	–	–	–	10.4	–	6.4	8.1
20-40 mph	8.9	–	8.5	9.3	10.4	6.7	6.6	8.3
30-50 mph	9.0	10.9	8.9	9.1	10.4	6.6	6.6	8.3
40-60 mph	9.8	11.4	9.6	9.3	11.8	6.3	6.4	8.6
50-70 mph	11.8	13.4	10.2	8.7	9.5	12.7	6.1	6.7
60-80 mph	14.6	13.7	10.9	10.2	13.3	6.6	7.4	9.5
70-90 mph	–	16.1	13.1	12.4	15.7	7.9	8.7	10.3
80-100 mph	–	–	19.4	22.5	22.9	9.6	10.9	11.8
90-110 mph	–	–	–	–	–	15.4	16.3	15.7
100-120 mph	–	–	–	–	–	–	–	–
110-130 mph	–	–	–	–	–	–	–	–
Overall fuel consumption (mpg)	23.7	25.8	23.1	26.5	25.2	22.6	21.4	21.6
Typical fuel consumption (mpg)	33	30	29	28	28	27	24	24
Kerb weight (lb)	1680	1540	1904	1624	1974	1988	2240	2562
Original test published	1961**	1961	1966**	1969	1976	1969**	1974	1980

** Tested by *Motor;* all other British tests by Autocar

* *Estimated speed in overdrive top gear*

	Convertible Turbo 2994cc 6-cyl Ford	Tuscan 4727cc V8 Ford USA	2500 2498cc 6-cyl Triumph	2500M 2498cc 6-cyl Triumph	Convertible 2994cc 6-cyl Ford	Tuscan 4949cc V8 (220 bhp) Ford USA	350i Series 2 3528cc V8 Rover	390SE 3905cc V8 Rover
Mean maximum speed (mph)	139	155***	111	109	125***	119****	136	144
Acceleration (sec)								
0-30 mph	2.4	2.5	3.4	3.0	2.6	2.8	2.5	2.3
0-40 mph	3.2	3.5	5.1	4.5	3.9	3.7	4.1	3.5
0-50 mph	4.5	4.5	7.5	6.6	5.7	4.8	5.0	4.5
0-60 mph	5.8	5.7	10.6	9.3	7.7	7.2	6.6	5.6
0-70 mph	7.2	7.5	14.2	12.8	10.7	10.2	9.3	7.8
0-80 mph	9.4	9.0	18.5	17.8	14.1	13.1	11.7	9.6
0-90 mph	11.5	10.8	–	25.3	18.8	–	14.6	12.3
0-100 mph	14.3	13.8	31.0	–	–	25.0	20.2	15.4
0-110 mph	18.2	16.8	–	–	–	–	23.0	19.0
0-120 mph	23.1	20.3	–	–	–	–	29.4	24.5
0-130 mph	31.3	–	–	–	–	–	–	35.8
Standing ¼-mile (sec)	14.5	14.1	17.7	17.3	16.6	15.4	14.8	14.3
Direct top gear (sec)								
10-30 mph	–	–	–	–	–	–	7.0	–
20-40 mph	8.2	5.0	–	–	–	–	6.3	5.3
30-50 mph	7.1	4.8	–	–	–	–	6.0	5.0
40-60 mph	6.8	4.9	–	–	–	–	5.9	4.9
50-70 mph	6.4	4.9	–	–	–	–	5.9	4.9
60-80 mph	5.7	4.9	–	–	–	–	5.8	4.9
70-90 mph	5.0	5.0	–	–	–	–	6.2	5.0
80-100 mph	5.3	5.6	5.3	5.6	–	–	7.2	5.1
90-110 mph	6.3	6.3	–	–	–	–	6.5	5.4
100-120 mph	8.3	6.9	–	–	–	–	10.6	6.2
110-130 mph	13.2	–	–	–	–	–	–	8.8
Overall fuel consumption (mpg)	17.7	16.1	–	–	–	–	19.6	21.3
Typical fuel consumption (mpg)	19	17	32	29	25	20	22	25
Kerb weight (lb)	2436	2274	2150	2275	2335	2240	2520	–
Original test published	1979	1967**	1973	1977	1978	1970	1985	1984

*** Estimated speed

**** Limited by 5200 rpm and axle gearing